Español Con Amigos

A Partner Approach to Basic Conversational Spanish

Melissa J. O'Gara

ACKNOWLEDGMENTS

Thanks to my ever-supportive husband, Michael, and to Katie and Michael Liam. A special thanks to the AFS program for, without it, I would never be able to write this text

Chapter 1: Meet and Greet

Greetings and Expressions of Courtesy

Saludos y Cortesía	Greetings and Courtesy
Hola	Hello
Buenos días	Good morning
Buenas tardes	Good afternoon
Buenas noches	Good evening
¿Cómo se llama Usted?	What is your name? (formal)
¿Cómo te llamas (tú)?	What is your name? (informal)
Me llamo … Mi nombre es … Yo soy…	My name is…
Mucho gusto.	Pleased to meet you.
Encantado (a).	Delighted
Igualmente.	Likewise.
Es un placer	It's a pleasure.
El gusto es mío.	The pleasure is mine.
¿Qué tal?	How's everything going?
¿Cómo está Usted?	How are you (formal)?
¿Cómo estás?	How are you (informal)?
¿Y Usted?	And you? (formal)
¿Y tú?	And you (informal)
¡Cuánto tiempo!	It's been a long while/ Long time no see!
¿Qué hay de nuevo?	What's new?
¿Qué pasa?	What's happening? / What's up?
Respuestas	**Answers**
(Estoy) muy bien, gracias	(I am) very well, thank you.

(to the left of "Me llamo" row) ✱

Estoy bien.	I'm well.
Así, así	So-so
Respuestas	**Answers**
Regular	Not so great
Sin novedades.	Not much happening./ No news. / Not much
Muy mal.	Very badly.
No mucho.	Nothing much.
Gracias.	Thank you.
De nada.	You're welcome.
No hay de qué.	Don't mention it. / You're welcome.
Por favor.	Please.
Despedidas	**Farewells**
Me voy	I'm leaving
Adiós	Goodbye
Chau	Ciao/ Bye for now
Nos vemos.	See you.
Hasta luego.	See you. / Bye/ Till then.
Hasta pronto.	See you soon.
Hasta la próxima.	See you next time.
Hasta la vista.	See you (when it's someone you don't know well and you don't know when you'll see him/her again.
Hasta el (lunes,martes,miércoles, jueves, viernes, sábado, domingo)	Until (Monday, Tuesday, Wednesday, Thursday, Friday, Saturday, Sunday)
Hablamos pronto.	Let's talk soon.
Estamos en contacto.	Let's be in touch.
Qué le vaya bien.	I wish you well. (formal)
Qué te vaya bien.	I wish you well. (informal)
Suerte.	Good luck.

Buen viaje.	Have a good trip.
Cuídate.	Take care (informal, with a friend)
Cuídese.	Take care (formal)

Diálogos (*Dialogues*)
As you read the conversations/dialogues in each section throughout this book, try to understand the meaning of the whole conversation. Some words or phrases may be new to you. It's okay if you don't know every word. Just try to catch the overall meaning. To check your understanding, see the English translation in the appendix.

Diálogo 1.1
Read aloud this conversation between two people of the same age.

Estudiante A – Buenos días.
Estudiante B – Buenos días. ¿Como te llamas?
Estudiante A – Me llamo Susana, ¿Y tú?
Estudiante B – Mucho gusto, Susana. Me llamo Carlos.
Estudiante A – Es un placer, Carlos.
Estudiante B – Igualmente. Nos vemos.
Estudiante A – Hasta luego, Carlos.

Diálogo 1.2
Now try this conversation between a teacher and a student.

Profesora: Buenas tardes, Mateo. ¿Cómo estás?
Estudiante: Estoy muy bien, gracias. ¿Y Ud.? ¿Qué tal?
Profesora: Así así. Tengo mucho trabajo.
Estudiante: Entonces, me voy. Qué le vaya bien, Señora.
Profesora: Muchas gracias, Mateo. Hasta el jueves.

Diálogo 1.3
Now you try! Write a brief conversation with your friend using the guidelines:

1. Greet each other.

2. Ask for each other's name.

3. Ask how your partner is and respond. (Don't forget to thank your partner!)

4. Ask if anything is new and respond.

5. Say goodbye to each other.

Chapter 2: Hey, Who Are You?

Describing Yourself; Saying Where You Are From; Stating Profession

Subject Pronouns

*To discuss people in Spanish, you will often use SUBJECT PRONOUNS (I, you, he, she, we, you all, they).

Los pronombres sujetos (Singular)	Subject Pronouns (Singular)		Los pronombres Sujetos (Plural)	Subject Pronouns Plural
Yo	I		Nosotros / Nosotras	We
Tú	You (informal)		Vosotros / Vosotras	You guys (informal – Spain only)
Usted (Ud.)	You (formal)		Ustedes (Uds.)	You all
Él	He		Ellos	They (boys + girls)
Ella	She		Ellas	They (girls only)

*We do not use the subject pronouns in Spanish as often as we do in English. Generally, the ending you choose for a verb will already let your listener or reader know who the subject is.

*The "vosotros/as" form is used to talk directly to two or more people you know well or can speak with informally. This form is used in Spain only. In most all other countries where Spanish is spoken, in order to talk to a group of people directly, we use the form "Uds.".

*Nosotros can mean "we" (a group of all males) or "we" (a group of males and females). "Nosotras" can only mean "we" (a group of females only). The same rule follows for "vosotros"/"vosotras" and "ellos"/"ellas". See the following chart:

Nosotros = we (boys and mixed)
Nosotras = we (girls)
Vosotros = you guys (boys and mixed)
Vosotras = you guys (all girls)

The Verb "Ser"

*To describe a person or explain who he or she is, use the verb "ser" ("to be").

Ser = to be			
Yo **soy**	*I am*	Nosotros/ Nosotras **somos**	*We are*
Tú **eres**	*You (informal) are*	Vosotros / Vosotras **sois**	*You guys (informal – Spain only)*
Ud. **es**	*You (formal) are*	Ustedes (Uds.) **son**	*You all*
Él **es**	*He is*	Ellos **son**	*They* *(boys + girls)*
Ella **es**	*She is*	Ellas **son**	*They (girls only)*

Ejemplos:

1. Ella es alta. = *She is tall.*

2. Soy una persona fuerte. = *I am a strong person.*

3. ¿Cómo eres? = *What are you (informal) like? (informal)*

4. Ud. es muy amable. = *You (formal) are very friendly.*

5. Uds. son estudiantes. = *You all are students.*

6. Sois interesantes. = *You guys (in Spain) are interesting.*

7. Somos amigos. = *We are friends.*

*Sometimes we don't use pronouns as subjects. We use a name or title instead. For example, instead of saying "she", we say, "Marta". Instead of saying "we", we say "Mateo and I".

Práctica 2.1:
Find the correct pronoun (yo, tú, él, ella, Ud., nosotros(as), vosotros(as), Uds., ellos ellas) to match the people named below:

1. Susana y Julia = _____ELLAS_____
2. Carlos = _____ÉL_____
3. You and José = _____USTEDES_____
4. Carolina and I = _____NOSOTRAS_____

Práctica 2.2
Now include the form of the verb "ser" that would match these subjects:

1. Susana y Julia are = <u>ELLAS SON</u>
2. Carlos is = <u>El es</u>
3. You and José are = <u>Ustedes son</u>
4. Carolina and I are = <u>Nosotros somos</u>

Stating Where Someone is From

*To ask someone where he/she is from, you use "De dónde" (From where):

¿De dónde eres (tú)?	Where are you (informal) from?
¿De dónde es Ud.?	Where are you (formal) from?
(Yo) Soy de..	I am from….

Ejemplos:

¿Eres tú de California? = *Are you from California?*

Sí, (yo) soy de Californa. = *Yes, I am from California*

No, (yo) no soy de California. = *No, I am not from California.*

Adjectives

*You already know a lot of Spanish! Listed below are some adjectives (descriptive words) that are also cognates (words that look similar in different languages and have the same meaning).

*Use the words in the list below with the verb "ser" to describe yourself and others!

*Adjectives must match the GENDER of the noun they describe (masculine or feminine gender). If you are a male, the ending is generally "o" and if you are female, the ending is "a". If the ending is not "o" or "a", there will be no change – you use the same ending for both masculine and feminine.

* Adjectives must also match in NUMBER with the noun they describe. If more than one thing or person is being described, you will add an "s" to the end of the word.

High-Frequency Adjectives

Activo (a)	Active
Amable	Amiable, friendly

Artístico (a)	Artistic
Atlético (a)	Athletic
Cómico (a)	Comical, funny
Conservativo (a)	Conservative
Contento (a)	Content, happy
Creativo (a)	Creative
Desobediente	Disobedient
Diferente	Different
Difícil	Difficult
Diligente	Diligent
Eficiente	Efficient
Energético (a)	Energetic
Estricto (a)	Strict
Estudioso (a)	Studious
Extrovertido (a)	Extroverted
Fabuloso (a)	Fabulous
Fotogénico (a)	Photogenic
Impaciente	Impatient
Inteligente	Intelligent
Interesante	Interesting
Introvertido (a)	Introverted
Liberal	Liberal
Maravilloso (a)	Marvelous
Obediente	Obedient
Paciente	Patient
Pensativo (a)	Pensive
Prudente	Prudent, cautious
Religioso (a)	Religious
Romántico (a)	Romantic
Serio (a)	Serious
Sincero (a)	Sincere

Talentoso (a)	Talented
Tímido (a)	Timid, shy
Tranquilo (a)	Tranquil, calm
Valiente	Brave, valiant

*To ask someone if he/she is romantic, shy, pensive, etc., use the form of the verb "ser" that matches your subject and put the adjective after. Be sure the ending of the adjective matches the person you're asking about.

Ejemplo: ¿Eres tranquilo? = *Are you tranquil (a tranquil person)?*
Ejemplo: ¿Son Uds. valientes? = *Are you all brave?*

*To answer a question affirmatively, say "Sí" and then the subject and verb.
Ejemplo: -¿Eres creativo, José? = *Are you creative, José?*
-Sí, soy creativo. = *Yes, I am creative.*

*To answer with "no" to a question, we need to say, "No" and then place another "no" before the verb.
Ejemplo: - ¿Son Uds. valientes? = *Are you all brave?*
- No, (nosotros) no somos valientes. = *No, we are **not** brave.*

Diálogo 2.1
Choose a role, and then read the following dialogue aloud to your partner.

Paco: Hola, Marta. ¿Cómo estás hoy?
Marta: Hola, Paco. Estoy bien. ¿Y tú?
Paco: Muy bien, gracias. Marta, ¿Cómo eres tú?
Marta: ¿Yo? Soy maravillosa, Paco.
Paco: Marta, en serio. ¿Cómo eres tú?
Marta: Bueno, soy paciente, energética, y muy amable. ¿Y tú, Paco? ¿Cómo eres?
Paco: Soy atlético, energético y extrovertido.
Marta: Y muy fotogénico, ¿no?
Paco: No, no soy fotogénico. Y, Marta, ¿Cómo son tus hijos?
Marta: Bueno, mi hijo es muy serio y estudioso. Mi hija es tímida y tranquila.
Paco: Gracias, Marta.
Marta: De nada.

Práctica 2.3
Tell a partner what you are like using the list above. Complete the sentence that starts with... "(Yo) soy..." by adding adjectives that describe you. Make sure your adjectives end with the proper vowel to match your gender. Note that "y" means "and".

1. Yo soy ___talentosa___, ___creativa___ y
___contenta___.

Práctica 2.4
Tell a partner what you are NOT like by using the list of adjectives. Complete the sentence that starts with … "(Yo) no soy…" by adding adjectives that DO NOT describe you. Note that "o" means "or".

1. Yo no soy _____ATHLÉTICO_____, _____TÍMIDO_____ o
_____FOTOGÉNICO_____

Práctica 2.5
Answer the following questions:

1. ¿Eres tú muy atlético(a)? _Yo no soy muy atletica_

2. ¿Eres tú obediente o desobediente? _YO SOY DESOBEDIENTE!_

3. ¿Eres tú muy prudente? _Yo no soy muy prudente._

4. ¿Eres tú cómico(a)? _Si, soy cómico_

5. ¿Es tu esposo(a) (spouse) creativo(a)? _Si, MI ESPOSA ES muy CREATIVA_

6. ¿Es tu ~~esposa~~ (a) paciente? _no, mi prima no es paciente_
   prima

7. ¿Es tu hermano(a) (brother/sister) amable? _Si. MI HERMANO JUAN ES muy AMABLE._

8. ¿Es tu ~~hermano~~(a) extrovertido(a)? _Si, mi hermano es muy extrovertido_
   primo

Stating Profession

When stating your profession, you may also need to change the ending of the word to match your gender.

> **Ejemplos:**
> Soy abogado. = *I am a (male) lawyer.*
> Soy abogada. = *I am a (female) lawyer.*

The endings "e" and "ista" match both genders.

> **Ejemplos:**
> Él es artista. = *He is an artist.*
> Ella es artista. = *She is an artist.*

9

*We don't say "a" or "an" when stating a profession unless there is an adjective added.

Ejemplos:
Soy profesora. = *I am a (female) teacher.*
Soy una profesora paciente. = *I am a patient (female) teacher.*

Questions About Professions

¿Cuál es tu profesión?	What is your (informal) profession?
¿Cuál es su profesión?	What is your (formal) profession?
¿Qué haces?	What do you (informal) do?
¿Qué hace Ud.?	What do you (formal) do?
¿Qué trabajo tienes?	What is your (informal) job?
¿Qué trabajo tiene (Ud.)?	What is your (formal) job?
¿Cuál es la profesión de …. (tu hermano, tu esposo/a, tus padres)?	What is (your brother's, your spouse's, your parents') profession?

Common Professions

Abogado (a)	Lawyer
Actor/ Actriz	Actor/ Actress
Amo (a) de casa	Homemaker
Agente de seguros	Insurance Agent
Agente de bienes raíces	Real Estate Agent
Agente de viajes	Travel Agent
Agente de facturación	Billing agent
Arquitecto (a)	Arquitect
Artista	Artist
Auditor (a)	Auditor
Audiólogo (a)	Audiologist
Autónomo (a)	Freelanceer/ self-employed
Auxiliar de vuelo	Flight Attendant
Banquero (a)	Banker
Bibliotecario (a)	Librarian

Bombero (a)	Firefighter
Camarero (a) / mozo (a)	Waiter
Cantante	Singer
Carpintero (a)	Carpenter
Cartero (a)	Mail carrier
Científico (a)	Scientist
Cocinero (a)	Cook
Comediante	Comedian
Conductor (a)	Driver
Contador (a)	Accountant
Consejero (a)	Counselor
Dentista	Dentist
Diseñador (a)	Designer
Doctor (a)	Doctor
Editor (a)	Editor
Electricista	Electrician
Enfermero (a)	Nurse
Escritor (a)	Writer
Farmacéutico (a)	Pharmacist
Físico (a)	Physicist
Fisioterapeuta	Physical Therapist
Fotógrafo (a)	Photographer
Funcionario (a)	Civil servant
Gerente	Manager
Granjero (a)	Farmer
Informático (a)	Computer scientist
Ingeniero (a)	Engineer
Jardinero (a)	Gardener
Jefe (a)	Boss
Jubilado (a) / Retirado (a) (Uses verb estar… estoy jubilado/a)	Retired (Estoy jubilado (a) = I am retired)
Juez (a)	Judge

Mecánico (a)	Mechanic
Médico (a)	Doctor
Músico (a)	Musician
Negociante	Business person
Oficinista	Clerk, Office Worker
Óptico (a)	Optician
Periodista	Journalist
Piloto (a)	Pilot
Pintor (a)	Painter
Plomero (a)	Plumber
Policía	Police Officer
Primer (a) cocinero (a)	Chef
Profesor (a)	Teacher, professor
Programador (a) de computadoras	Computer Programmer
Psicólogo (a)	Psychologist
Psiquiatra	Psychiatrist
Recepcionista	Receptionist
Reportero (a)	Reporter
Sacerdote	Priest
Secretario (a)	Secretary
Técnico (a)	Technician
Terapeuta	Therapist
Traductor (a)	Translator
Vendedor (a)	Vendor/ Salesperson
Veterinario (a)	Veterinarian

Práctica 2.6
Complete these sentences with the professions of each person.

1. Soy <u>estudiante</u>

2. Mi papá es/era (*is/was*) <u>negociante</u>

3. Mi mamá es/era (*is/was*) <u>maestra</u>

4. Mi esposo (a) es _traductor_

5. Mi mejor amigo (a) es _estudiante_

6. Mi compañero (a) de clase es _estudiante_

Diálogo 2.2

Choose one partner to be "Estudiante A" and the other to play the role of "Estudiante B". Practice by reading your part aloud. Choose the endings that match your own gender.

Estudiante A – Hola, ¿Qué tal?

Estudiante B – Bien, gracias. ¿Y tú?

Estudiante A – Así, así. Fue un día muy largo. Soy científico(a). Hay mucho trabajo. ¿Cuál es tu profesión?

Estudiante B – Soy banquero(a). Eres muy inteligente, ¿no? Es difícil ser científico(a).

Estudiante A – Sí. Es difícil. Bueno, nos vemos en clase el próximo jueves.

Estudiante B – Muy bien. Hasta luego.

Estudiante A – Chao.

Diálogo 2.3

Choose one partner to be "Estudiante A" and the other to play the role of "Estudiante B". Practice by reading your part aloud. Choose the endings that match your own gender.

Estudiante A – Buenas noches, (Señor/Señorita/Señora). ¿Cómo se llama Usted?

Estudiante B – Buenas noches. Me llamo (Señor/Señorita/Señora + (your last name)

Estudiante A – Es un placer, (Señor/Señorita/Señora + (your partner's last name).

Estudiante B - Igualmente. ¿Y cómo se llama Usted?

Estudiante A – Mi nombre es (Señor/Señorita/Señora + (your last name).

Estudiante B - ¿Cuál es su profesión?

Estudiante A – Soy profesor(a).

Estudiante B - ¡Qué interesante! Ud. es muy paciente, ¿no?

Estudiante A – Ja, ja, ja... sí soy muy paciente. Gracias.

Estudiante B – Yo soy negociante y no soy muy paciente, pero soy muy pensativo(a) y prudente.

Estudiante A – Ud. es muy amable.

Estudiante B – Gracias. Fue un placer. Qué le vaya bien.

Estudiante A – Igualmente. Adiós.

Diálogo 2.4 (For three people)

Choose one partner to be "Estudiante A", another to play the role of "Estudiante B", and a third to play "Estudiante C". Practice by reading your part aloud. Choose the endings that match your own gender.

Estudiante A - Hola, amigo(a). ¿Cómo estás?

Estudiante B - Estoy así así. Te presento a mi hijo(a), (name of partner C).

Estudiante A – Mucho gusto.

Estudiante C – El gusto es mío.

Estudiante A – Tu hijo (a) es muy amable, ¿no?

Estudiante B – Mi hija(o) es muy desobediente.

Estudiante C – Papá(Mamá), no soy desobediente. Tú eres imposible y demasiado(a) estricto(a).

Estudiante B – No soy estricto(a). Soy muy paciente.

Estudiante A – Uds. dos son muy diferentes, ¿no?

Estudiante C – Sí. Mi papá (mamá) es muy diferente de mí.

Estudiante B -Mi hijo(a) es muy inteligente, talentoso(a), y creativo(a), pero no es obediente.

Estudiante A - Todas las familias son iguales. Es cierto. Bueno, suerte a Uds. dos. Me voy.

Estudiante B – Chao, amigo(a). Hasta la próxima.

Chapter 3: The ABC's of Español

The Spanish Alphabet and Rules of Pronunciation

*The alphabet in Spanish is useful for pronouncing all words since the sounds don't change as they do in English. They remain consistent. Learn the sounds and you can pronounce and spell all words.

Letra (Letter)	Sonido (sound)	Descripción (Description)	Palabras (Words)
A	Ah	The doctor says, "say ahhh." Short and quick.	papa, Ana, aguacate, amarillo
B	Be	Boy (when at the beginning of a word) (Lips are relaxed and sound is soft when it's within a word. Like a "v" without the vibration)	bola, habilidad, hablar, habana
C	Ce	Cent, cemetery, cylinder (when c is before I or e) Cat, coat, cute (before any letter except I or e)	centavo, cero, cielo, ciclo colina, cómodo, cuando, cabo
Ch	Che	Check, chick, nacho	chimichanga, cha cha cha
D	De	Deck (when at the beginning of a word) Thick (when between two vowels or at the end of the word. Your tongue should be between your teeth)	diablo, demasiado, de verdad, dedo, lealtad
E	Eh	Ehhh. Short and quick.	elefante, estirar, estrés
F	Efe	fight	fácil, fantástico, jirafa
G	Ge	hey, house, ha (when g is before I or e) gate, go, gum (before any letter except I or e)	genio, ingeniero, gimnasio grande, gota, igualmente
H	Hache	Never pronounce the h. It is always silent	hay, hola, habilidad, hablador
I	I	Eeek. (short and quick)	iba, igual, indio, ilegal
J	Jota	Hello (the h in hello)	jovial, hija, joven
K	Ka	Kite (like k in kite)	kimono, kilo

L	Ele	Like (like l in like)	lástima, hola, lápiz, lengua
LL	Elle	Yes (like y in yes)	ella, llamó, amarillo, valle
M	Eme	make (like m in make)	mamá, martes, música
N	Ene	Not (like n of not)	número, ni, nariz
Ñ	Eñe	Onion (like nio in onion)	cañón, cañada, señora
O	O	Ohhh! (short and quick)	los, abierto, otro
P	Pe	Pie (like p in pie)	preparar, trepar, poner
Q	Cu	K (like k in kite)	que, quien, química
R	Ere	Ladder (like the dd in ladder) Strong trill if initial	enero, hermano, pariente radio, restaurante, rodilla
Rr	Erre	Strongly trilled (never found at the beginning of the word)	ferrocarril, perro, carro
S	Ese	say (like s in say)	sola, salud, sencillo
T	Te	tough (like t in tough)	tela, estudiar, tocar
U	U	you (like the "ou" of you)	mucho, estudio, blusa
V	Ve	Boy (sounds like the b of boy)	violeta, vamos, uva
W	Doble u	Wall (found in only words brought from other languages)	Washington
X	Equis	ex (like x when when it's between vowels) sell (when it comes before a consonant)	exacto, extraordinario
Y	I griega	eager (like "ea" of eager when it's by itself) Yes (like y of yes in any other place)	y yo, yerno
Z	Zeta	cent (like c of cent)	zoológico, lápiz, nariz

Las Vocales – The Vowels	
A	Ah (Open your mouth and say ahh for the doctor)
E	Eh (As in "Eh? I can't hear a word you're saying.")
I	Eeeek, (As in, "Eeek" it's dark in here!")
O	Ohhhh (As in "Oh, my!")
U	You (as in "Hey You – go study these sounds!")

Syllables and Pronunciation

*Since Spanish was spoken before any written form came along, the writing was created to match how a word was spoken. There are patterns to the language, and the written accent mark was created so the word would read as it sounds. Listed below are the rules of pronunciation.

*Words that end in a vowel or "n" or "s" have the stress of the word on the second to the last syllable:

Práctica 3.1
Draw a circle around the second to the last syllable of the following words. Then practice stressing the syllable circled by saying the words aloud (your voice will trail upward a bit on the circled part of the word).

aduana: a/dua/na	colina: co/li/na	foto: fo/to
casa: ca/sa	hablan: ha/blan	tocas: to/cas
estudio: es/tu/dio	martes: mar/tes	vecinos: ve/ci/nos
bailas: bai/las	picante: pi/can/te	salsa: sal/sa

*Words that end in a consonant except "n" or "s" have the stress on the last syllable

Práctica 3.2
Draw a circle around the last syllable of the following words. Then practice stressing the syllable circled by saying the words aloud (your voice will trail upward a bit on the circled part of the word).

abril: a/bril	tomar: to/mar	ayudar: ay/u/dar
estudiar: es/tu/diar	nariz: na/riz	verdad: ver/dad
pared: pa/red	caracol: ca/ra/col	salud: sa/lud

*Words that don't follow this rule have an accent mark written over the vowel where the stress belongs. If a word is not pronounced according to the rule above, a written accent must be placed over a vowel in the syllable that should be stressed. Remember, the written language was trying to match the spoken; you have to know how a word is pronounced in order to know if an accent mark is needed. But the reader will know not to pronounce the word according to its spelling; the reader sees the accent mark and knows where the stressed syllable is.

Práctica 3.3

Draw a circle around the syllable with the accent mark. Note that the accent mark is placed in a location other than where the stress should be based upon the rules listed above. Practice stressing the syllable circled by saying the words aloud (your voice will trail upward a bit on the circled part of the word).

lápiz: lá/piz	fácil: fá/cil	mecánico: me/cá/ni/co
música: mú/si/ca	lámpara: lám/pa/ra	rincón: rin/cón
histórico: hi/stó/ri/co	sofá: so/fá	fantástico: fan/tás/ti/co
marrón: ma/rrón	calcetín: cal/ce/tín	mamá: ma/má
Martínez: Mar/tí/nez	papá: pa/pá	teléfono: te/lé/fo/no

*Single syllable words don't have accent marks unless there is another word spelled the same way that has a different meaning:

> **Sí**=yes; **si**=if   **él**=he; **el**=the   **tú**=you; **tu**=your

*The only other time accent marks are needed are to separate a weak vowel from a strong vowel.

- Strong vowels are "A", "E" and "O"

- Weak vowels are "I" and "U"

  (A trick to help you remember: *"U" and "I" are weak and everyone else is strong.)

*When two strong vowels are together, they stand alone on their own and take their own sound:

Ejemplos:

Leer = Le/er	Crea – cre/a	Veo – ve/o	Mateo = Ma/te/o

*When two weak vowels are together, they lean on each other and produce one sound.

Ejemplos:

Quien = quien	Cuidado= cui/da/do	Ciudad= ciu/dad	Suiza = sui/za

*When a weak and strong vowel are together, the weak leans on the strong.

Ejemplos:

Cuando = cuan/do	piano= pia/no	labio= la/bio	reina = rei/na

*BUT...when a weak vowel is paired with a strong vowel, and the weak vowel is pronounced with its own sound, we give the weak vowel an accent mark to separate it from the strong vowel.

Ejemplos:

María = Ma/rí/a   leíste = le/ís/te   río = rí/o   biología = bi/o/lo/gí/a

Práctica 3.4

Circle the syllable that would be stressed in each of the following words. Then, say the words aloud with your partner. Listen to your partner to make sure the main force of the word he/she says is on the circled syllable.

1. que – ma – do

2. e – lec- trón

3. ac – tua – li – dad

4. pan – ta – lla

5. al – ta – voz

6. es- ta – ción

7. ho – gar

8. es – ti – lo

9. ba – su- ra

10. fe – roz

11. va – lien –te

12. es – pe – cial

13. to – mas

14. es – ca – le – ra

15. es – tó – ma - go

Práctica 3.5

First, answer the question about yourself. Write "sí" in the column "yo" if the statement is true about you; write "no" in the "yo" column if it is not true about you. Afterwards, ask your partner the question. Record his/her response in the column "mi compañero/a". Try using complete sentences in your oral responses.

Ejemplo:
Estudiante A - ¿Eres (tú) muy inteligente?
Estudiante B – Sí, ¡(yo) soy muy inteligente!

Ejemplo:
Estudiante A - ¿Es tu compañero/a de clase impaciente?
Estudiante B – No, mi compañero/a de clase no es impaciente.

Pregunta	Yo	Mi compañero/a
1. ¿Eres (tú) estudiante?		
2. ¿Eres (tú) muy serio/a?		
3. ¿Eres (tú) de los Estados Unidos?		
4. ¿Eres (tú) muy creativo/a?		
5. ¿Es tu familia muy atlética?		
6. ¿Es tu familia muy amable?		
7. ¿Es tu esposo/a muy paciente?		
8. ¿Hay (Is there) un/a abogado/a en tu familia?		
9. ¿Hay un/a profesor/a en tu familia?		
10. ¿Son muy amables los estudiantes en la clase?		
11. ¿Eres (tú) una persona muy prudente?		
12. ¿Eres (tú) un/a conductor/a bueno/a?		
13. ¿Eres (tú) músico/a?		
14. ¿Es tu casa muy grande?		
15. ¿Es tu coche muy rápido?		

Chapter 4: What's Your Pleasure?
EXPRESSING LIKES/DISLIKES

* To say that someone likes an activity or item, we use one of the following phrases.

Expresar las preferencias	Expressing preferences
Me gusta + verb or singular noun	*I like*
Te gusta + verb or singular noun	*You like*
Le gusta + verb or singular noun	*You (formal), he, she likes*
Nos gusta + verb or singular noun	*We like*
Os gusta + verb or singular noun	*You guys like (Spain only)*
Les gusta + verb or singular noun	*You all, they like*

Ejemplos:
1. *I like to swim.* = Me gusta nadar.

2. *I like the book.* = Me gusta el libro.

3. *She likes to cook.* = Le gusta cocinar.

4. *We like the class.* = Nos gusta la clase.

5. *You like to read.* = Te gusta leer.

6. *Do you (formal) like to sing?* = ¿Le gusta cantar?

*To say that someone DOESN'T LIKE to do something or doesn't like some thing, you simply put "no" before the phrases listed above.

Ejemplos:
1. *I don't like to swim.* = No me gusta nadar.

2. *I don't like the book.* = No me gusta el libro.

3. *She doesn't like to cook.* = No le gusta cocinar.

4. *We don't like the class.* = No nos gusta la clase.

5. *You don't like to read.* = No te gusta leer.

6. *You (formal) don't like to sing?* = ¿No le gusta cantar?

*To say that someone likes (or doesn't like) more than one thing, we add "n" to the verb "gusta". Note that the English translation is the same.

Me gustan + Plural noun	*I like*
Te gustan + Plural noun	*You like*
Le gustan + Plural noun	*You (formal), he, she likes*
Nos gustan + Plural noun	*We like*
Os gustan + Plural noun	*You guys like (Spain only)*
Les gustan + Plural noun	*You all, they like*

Ejemplos:
1. *I like the books.* = Me gustan los libros.
2. *She likes the classes.* = Le gustan las clases.
3. *You (informal) like movies.* = Te gustan las películas
4. *They like the cars.* = Les gustan los carros.
5. *We like dogs.* = Nos gustan los perros.
6. *They don't like the animals.* = No les gustan los animales.

Likes and Dislikes

Pasatiempos Populares	**Popular Pastimes**
Construir	To build
Charlar	To Chat
Colectar	To collect
Cocinar	To cook
Bailar	To dance
Hacer trabajo	To do work
Dibujar	To draw
Comer	To eat
Entretener	To entertain
Hacer ejercicio	To exercise

Ir de compras	To go shopping
Ir al gimnasio	To go to the gym
Escuchar música	To listen to music
Pintar	To paint
Jugar (a)	To play
Tocar (un instrumento)	To play an instrument
Practicar deportes	To practice sports
Leer	To read
Andar en bicicleta	To ride a bike
Correr	To run
Cantar	To sing
Patinar	To skate
Andar en patineta	To skateboard
Esquiar	To ski
Pasar tiempo con amigos	To spend time with friends
Nadar	To swim
Dar un paseo	To take a walk
Sacar fotos	To take pictures
Hablar por teléfono	To talk on the phone
Viajar	To travel
Usar la computadora	To use the computer
Mirar la televisión	To watch television
Escribir	To write

Práctica 4.1
Complete the sentences by naming three different activities you like to do.

1. Me gusta _CANTAR_

2. Me gusta _ANDAR EN PATINETA_

3. Me gusta _PINTAR_

23

Complete the senteces by naming two activities you do <u>not</u> like to do:

1. No me gusta _HACER EJERCICIO_

2. No me gusta _deportes_

Práctica 4.2

Now ask your partner if he/she likes the activities you named in Práctica 4.1.
Notes before you begin this exercise:
*You may want to comment with "¡<u>Yo también!</u>" (*Me too!) *or "<u>Ni yo tampoco.</u>" (*Me neither*).
*When it's your turn to respond, you say either, "Sí, me gusta …" or "No, no me gusta…"
*If you want to say that you like something a lot, use "Me gusta mucho…"

1.   ¿Te gusta _____?

2.   ¿Te gusta _____?

3.   ¿Te gusta _____?

4.   ¿Te gusta _____?

5.   ¿Te gusta _____?

Activities and Pastimes

Deportes y Actividades Populares	Popular Sports and Activities
El béisbol	Baseball
El baloncesto	Basketball
El boxeo	Boxing
El fútbol americano	Football
El golf	Golf
El hockey	Hockey
El patinaje	Skating
El fútbol	Soccer
El surfing	Surfing
El tenis	Tennis
El voleibol	Volleyball
El esquí acuático	Water skiing

Práctica 4.3

Choose some of the activities/sports listed above or some of the activities mentioned in the previous section, and ask your partner if he/she likes them.

1. ¿Te gusta _____?

2. ¿Te gusta _____?

3. ¿Te gusta _____?

A Few Favorite and Not-So-Favorite Things

Una Variedad de Cosas	A Variety of Items
Los animales	Animals
El arte	Art
Los carros / los coches	Cars
Los gatos	Cats
Las ciudades	Cities
Las comedias	Comedies
Las computadoras	Computers
Los cruceros	Cruises
Los perros	Dogs
El pescado	Fish (the kind you eat)
Los peces	Fish (the kind that's still swimming!)
Las flores	Flowers
Los caballos	Horses
Las revistas	Magazines
Las películas	Movies
Las pinturas	Paintings
Los museos	Museums
La música	Music
Los periódicos	Newspapers
Los aviones	Planes
Los deportes	Sports
Los exámenes	Tests
La playa	The beach

El campo	The country
Los fines de semana	The weekends
El teatro	Theater
Las verduras	Vegetables
Los videojuegos	Video games
El trabajo	Work

Práctica 4.4
Decide with your partner who will be Estudiante A and who will be Estudiante B. Then, ask your partner the questions listed under your column. Have your partner respond using complete sentence answers.

Estudiante A
1. ¿Te gusta la música clásica?
2. ¿Te gustan los museos?
3. ¿Te gusta viajar?
4. ¿Te gustan los animales?
5. ¿Te gusta el boxeo?

Estudiante B
1. ¿Te gusta la música de rock?
2. ¿Te gustan las películas?
3. ¿Te gusta leer?
4. ¿Te gustan los perros?
5. ¿Te gusta el fútbol americano?

Práctica 4.5
Translate the sentences to Spanish.

1. He doesn't like vegetables.

_____

2. We don't like the beach.

_____

3. They don't like to sing.

_____

4. Do you all like soccer?

_____

5. She likes (the weekends).

_____

6. He likes (the) music.

_____

Adding Clarity or Emphasis When Expressing Likes and Dislikes

*A note about the sentences you just translated… When you said, "Le gustan los fines de semana", we had to know about whom we were talking. "Le gustan" can translate as "he likes," "she likes", and even "You (formal) like". So sometimes we need to clarify who it is we're talking about. Here's how we can clarify who it is that likes something. We add "a" and a pronoun or name. See the chart below:

A mí me gusta(n)	**A nosotros(as)** nos gusta(n)
A ti te gusta(n)	**A vosotros(as)** os gusta(n)
A él le gusta(n) or **A (person's name) le gusta(n)**... A Juan le gusta(n)	**A ellos** les gusta(n) or **A (person's name) y a (person's name)** **les gusta(n)**... A Juan y a Marta les gusta(n)
A ella le gusta(n) or **A (person's name) le gusta(n)**... *Ejemplo*: A Marta le gusta(n)...	**A Ellas** les gusta(n) or **A (person's name) y a (person's name)** **les gusta(n)**... *Ejemplo*: A Marta y a Carolina les gusta(n)
A Ud. le gusta(n)	**A Uds.** les gusta(n)

*Note: If you say "A mí me gustan los animales" it's emphasizing the word "I"… as in You don't like animals? Well, **I** like them! You are not changing the English translation. You are just adding more emphasis or clarity to the statement – making it very clear **who** it is that likes these things.

Práctica 4.6
Translate the following sentences to Spanish. Add the emphasis or clarity.

1. Tomás likes to swim =

_____

2. He likes to play basketball =

_____

3. Do you (Ud.) like to travel? =

_____

4. My friends like to read. =

_____

5. My husband likes to cook, but I like to eat! =

_____

* To say you like to do something or you like something A LOT, just put "mucho" after the word "gusta(n)":.

Ejemplos:

1. A él le gusta mucho leer. = *He likes reading a lot.*

2. Nos gusta mucho el español. = *We like Spanish a lot.*

3. Me gustan mucho los animales. = *I like animals a lot.*

* To say you LOVE to do something or you LOVE something (but not a person), replace "gusta(n)" with "encanta(n)".

Ejemplos:

1. Me encanta cantar. = *I love to sing.*

2. A ella le encantan los cruceros. = *She loves cruises.*

*Fascina(n) (*to fascinate*), **Importa(n)** (*to be important*), **interesa(n)** (*to interest*), and **molestar** (*to bother*) are verbs that work the same way the verb "gustar" does.

Práctica 4.7 :
Answer the following questions about yourself:

1. ¿Qué te encanta? _____

2. ¿Qué te fascina? _____

3. ¿Qué te interesa? _____

4. ¿Qué te molesta? _____

Práctica 4.8
Now ask your partner the questions from above and see if you share any of the same answers!

Diálogo 4.1 – La primera cita (the first date)
Choose a role, and then read the following dialogue aloud to your partner.

Tomás – Hola, Marta, ¿Qué tal?

Marta - Bien, Tomás, gracias. Y gracias por invitarme a este restaurante.

Tomás – Es un placer, Marta. Me gustaría conocerte mejor.

Marta – Igualmente, Tomás.

Tomás – Bueno, entonces. ¿Qué te gusta hacer en tu tiempo libre?

Marta - ¡Uf! ¡Mucho! Me gusta mucho leer y pasar tiempo con mis amigos. No me gusta dibujar, pero me interesa el arte. Me gusta escuchar música – ¡ay!, y me encanta jugar deportes. Pero no me gusta mirar los deportes. ¿Y a ti, Tomás? ¿Qué te gusta hacer?

Tomás – A mí me gustan los deportes también. Pero, a mí me gusta mirar los deportes en la tele. Me gusta cocinar y me gustan los programas de cocina.

Marta - ¿Te interesan los programas de historia? A mí me encantan.

Tomás - Sí, me gusta mucho la historia. Pero me molestan los programas de historia. Son muy aburridos. Prefiero leer la historia de libros históricos.

Marta – Eres muy interesante, Tomás. Tenemos mucho en común.

Diálogo 4.2 – Vecinos nuevos (New Neighbors)
Choose a role, and then read the following dialogue aloud to your partner. (Vecino/a = neighbor)

Vecina #1 – Buenos días. Yo soy tu vecina nueva, Marisa. Mucho gusto.

Vecina #2 – Mucho gusto, Marisa. Me llamo Alisa.   Bienvenida a la vecindad.

Vecina #1 – Gracias, Alisa. Dime…¿tienes una familia?

Vecina #2 – Sí, mi esposo, mis tres hijos, y yo. Y dos perros también. ¿Y tú? ¿Tienes familia?

Vecina #1 – Sí, mi esposo, mis dos hijos, y yo. Y un gato muy desagradable. No me gusta el gato, pero a mis hijos les encanta.

Vecina #2 – Ja, ja, ja. A mis hijos les encanta todo tipo de animal. ¿Qué les interesa a tus hijos? ¿Les gustan los videojuegos?

Vecina #1 – Sí, les fascinan. Pero a mí no me gustan. Para ellos, prefiero los deportes. A ellos les gusta jugar deportes y es más saludable, ¿no crees?

Vecina #2 – Claro que sí. A toda mi familia le gustan los deportes también. ¿Y a ti? ¿Te gusta leer? Hay un club de lectores donde hablamos de vez en cuando de los libros contemporáneos. ¿Te interesa un club así?

Vecina #1 – Sí, me interesa mucho. Me encanta leer.

Vecina #2 - ¡Qué bueno!

Práctica 4.9

Now, write a few questions you'd like to know about your partner. Then, ask them those questions. Here are some ideas:

1. ¿Te interesa el arte?
2. ¿Te interesan los museos?
3. ¿Qué te gusta más, leer o escribir?
4. ¿Te molestan los niños (little kids)?
5. ¿Te molestan los animales?
6. ¿Te gusta mucho viajar?
7. ¿Cómo te gusta viajar? ¿En avión, en tren, en carro o a pie (by foot)?
8. ¿Qué te gusta hacer los fines de semana?

interesa
interesan

Práctica 4.10

Translate the following dialogue to Spanish. Then, act it out with your partner.

Estudiante A – Hi, (fill in name of partner). How are you?

HOLA, CHILIS, QUE TAL

Estudiante B – Hi, (fill in name of partner). I'm doing well, thank you. What's up?

HOLA, INADPY. ESTOY BIEN, GRACIAS. QUE TAL

Estudiante A – Nothing much. (Name of partner), are you interested in art?

NO MUCH, CHIS, TE INTRESA EL ARTE?

Estudiante B – Yes, art fascinates me! I like it a lot.

SI, ME INTRESA EL ARTE, ME GUSTA MUCHO

Estudiante A – Well, in the Norton Simon Museum, there is a painting (una pintura) by (por) Diego Rivera. Do you like the paintings by Diego Rivera?

EN EL MUSEO DE N.S, HAY UNA PINTURA POR D.R. TE GUSTA LAS PINTRAS DE DIEGO RIVERA

Estudiante B – Yes, I love them!

SI, ME ENCANTAN LAS.

30

Chapter 5: Person, Place or Thing?

Stating What Something Is (Articles and Nouns)

*Nouns name people, animals, places or things.

*All Spanish nouns have masculine or feminine gender. The gender of nouns must be learned/memorized. When you learn a new noun, learn it with its "article", the word "the".

el los
la las

*Nouns ending in –o are usually (but not always) masculine

*Nouns ending in –a are usually (but not always) feminine

*When nouns identify one item, they are singular. When they identify more than one item, they are plural.

*In Spanish, the words "the", "a", "an", and "some" also have to match the noun they go with in gender and number.

*The following all mean "the". We choose the one that matches the gender and number of the noun we are describing.

Masculine Singular	**el** *(the)*	Chico *(boy)*
Masculine Plural	**los** *(the)*	Chicos *(boys)*

Feminine Singular	**La** *(the)*	Chica *(girl)*
Feminine Plural	**Las** *(the)*	Chicas *(girls)*

Práctica 5.1

Fill in with the correct article, the correct word for "the"

1. the dresses = __los__ vestidos
2. the shirts = __las__ camisas
3. the jacket = __La__ chaqueta
4. the t-shirts = __las__ camisetas
5. the sunglasses = __el__ gafas de sol
6. the blouses = __las__ blusas
7. the hat = __El__ sombrero
8. the shoes = __los__ zapatos
9. the ring = __El__ anillo
10. the purse = __la__ bolsa

*The following words mean "a", "an" or "some".

Masculine Singular	un (a)	Chico (boy)
Masculine Plural	unos (some)	Chicos (boys)

Feminine Singular	una (a)	Chica (girl)
Feminine Plural	unas (some)	Chicas (girls)

Práctica 5.2

Fill in with the correct indefinite article, the word for "a", "an", or "some" and the noun.

1. some dresses = ___UNOS___ ___JESTIOOS___

2. some shirts = ___UNAS___ ___CAMYSAS___

3. a jacket ___UN___ ___CHAQUETA___

4. a blouse = ___UNA___ ___BLUSA___

5. a hat = ___UN___ ___SOMBRERO___

6. some shoes = ___UNOS___ ___ZAPATOS___

7. a t-shirt = ___UNA___ ___CAMISETA___

8. some rings = ___UNOS___ ___ANILLOS___

9. a purse = _____ _____

10. some sunglasses = _____ _____

Práctica 5.3
Repeat the words below and then answer the questions that follow.

1. la lámpara

2. la cama

3. el teléfono

4. el enchufe

5. la bañera / la ducha

6. el secador de pelo

7. el termostato

8. el sillón y el otomano

9. la lavadora

10. la secadora

11. el despertador

12. el basurero y la basura

13. la pintura

14. el televisor

15. el sofá

16. la bombilla

Práctica 5.4

Choose one partner to ask the odd numbered questions and the other ask the even numbered questions. Help your partner answers in a complete sentence as the "ejemplos" demonstrate.

Ejemplos:

1. ¿Qué es esto? Es la lámpara?

No, no es la lámpara. Es la cama.

2. ¿Qué es esto? Es el enchufe?

Sí, es el enchufe.

1. ¿Qué es esto? ¿Es el teléfono?

2. ¿Qué es esto? ¿Es la cama?

3. ¿Qué es esto? ¿Es el enchufe?

4. ¿Qué es esto? ¿Es el secador de pelo?

5. ¿Qué son estos? ¿Es el basurero y la basura?

6. ¿Qué es esto? ¿Es el televisor?

Práctica 5.5

Repeat the words below. Note the use of the indefinite articles ("a", "an", "some") instead of the defininte article ("the").

1. un teatro

2. un correo

3. unos carros/coches

4. un estacionamiento

5. una farmacia

6. un cajero electrónico

7. una estación de policía

8. un restaurante

9. una estación de tren

10. un autobús

11. una tienda

12. un edificio

13. una carretera

14. una ciudad

15. una estación de gasolina

16. un hotel

Práctica 5.6

Choose one partner to ask the odd numbered questions and the other ask the even numbered questions. Help your partner answers in a complete sentence as the "ejemplos" demonstrate.

Ejemplos:

1. ¿Es una estación de tren?

No, no es una estación de tren. Es un teatro.

2. ¿Es un hotel?

Sí, es un hotel.

1. ¿Es un restaurante?

2. ¿Es un edificio?

3. ¿Es una carretera?

4. ¿Es un estacionamiento?

5. ¿Es una estación de gasolina?

6. ¿Son unos carros?

Práctica 5.7

Repeat the words below. Note the use of the indefinite articles ("a", "an", "some") instead of the defininte article ("the").

1. un tenedor

2. una silla

3. una servilleta y un tenedor

4. la botella de vino

5. un cuchillo

6. una mesa

7. una cuchara

8. la comida

9. un vaso

10. el baño

11. una taza

12. la cuenta

13. el plato

14. el camarero/el mozo

15. el menú

16. la camarera/la moza

Práctica 5.8

Choose one partner to ask the odd numbered questions and the other ask the even numbered questions. Help your partner answers in a complete sentence as the "ejemplos" demonstrate.

Ejemplos:

1.¿Quién es? ¿Es el policía?
   No, no es el policía. Es el camarero.

2.¿Qué es esto?

   Es un plato.

1.¿Qué es esto?

2. ¿Quién es? ¿Es la profesora?

3. ¿Qué son estos?

4. ¿Qué es esto?

5. ¿Qué es esto?

6.¿Qué es esto?

Note: Did you notice that it was easier to remember/recall these words than it was to recall words from the vocabulary lists in previous chapters? Can you guess the reason? When your learn vocabulary from something visual, it's often easier to remember. Keep this in mind while you practice what you've learned here. You might want to label items in your house with the Spanish vocabulary word. Watch TV in Spanish and use the subtitle option if you can. This way, you learn the words while you see them and you'll have an easier time remembering the new vocabulary!

Chapter 6: Gimme The Details

Describing What Something Is Like (Adjectives)

* Adjectives describe nouns

* Adjectives usually go AFTER a noun in Spanish. We name the item and then describe it.

* Adjectives must also match in gender and number with the noun they describe.

* If the adjective ends with a vowel, except for "e", we need to use the ending "o" or "os" for masculine nouns and "a" or "as" to describe feminine nouns. The ending "e" and all consonants agree with both genders.

* To make an adjective plural, just add "s" to the end of the word. If the word ends in a consonant, add "es"

* Colors and nationalities are adjectives.

Ejemplos:

1. *The red dress* = el vestid**o** roj**o**   5. *the green skirt* = la fald**a** verd**e**

2. *The black hats* = los sombr**eros** ne**gros**   6. *the green sweater* = el suéte**r** verd**e**

3. *the yellow blouses* = las blus**as** amarill**as**   7. *the blue sock* = el calcetí**n** azu**l**

4. *The orange shirt* = la camis**a** anaranjad**a**   8. *the blue t-shirts* = las camiset**as** azul**es**

The Colors

Los Colores	The Colors
Rojo	Red
Azul	Blue
Amarillo	Yellow
Blanco	White
Marrón / café / pardo	Brown
Negro	Black
Rosado	Pink
Verde	Green
Anaranjado	Orange
Morado	Purple

Gris	Gray
Color + claro ... (azul claro, verde claro)	Light color ... (light blue, light green)
Color + oscuro ... (azul oscuro, verde oscuro)	Dark color ... (dark blue, dark green)

Useful Expressions With Colors

Preguntas Útiles	Useful Questions
¿De qué color es/son...?	What color is/are ... ?
¿Cómo es?; ¿Cómo eres?; ¿Cómo son?	What is it like?; What are you like?; What are they like?

Ejemplo:

1. ¿De qué color es el vestido? = *What color is the dress?*
2. El vestido es rojo. = *The dress is red.*
3. Es un vestido rojo. = *It is a red dress.*

Práctica 6.1
Answer the following questions about colors.

1. Si te gusta llevar el color negro, ¿eres una persona cómica o seria?

   - Si me gusta llevar el color negro, soy una persona _____

2. Si te gusta el color verde, ¿eres impaciente o paciente?

   - Si me gusta el color verde, soy _____

3. Si tu color favorito es rojo, ¿eres extrovertido o introvertido?

   - Si mi color favorito es rojo, soy _____

4. ¿De qué color es tu casa (house)?

   - Mi casa es _____

5. ¿De qué color es tu cocina (kitchen)?

   - Mi cocina es _____

6. ¿De qué color es tu dormitorio (bedroom)?

   -Mi dormitorio es _____

7. ¿De qué color es tu carro (car)?

   - Mi carro es _____

8. ¿De qué color son tus ojos (eyes)?

   - Mis ojos son _____

9. ¿De qué color son tus zapatos?

   - Mis zapatos son_____

10. ¿Cuál es tu color favorito?

   - Mi color favorito es _____

Antonyms

Difícil	Hard
Fácil	Easy
Grande	Big
Pequeño (a)	Small
Corto (a)	Short (length)
Largo (a)	Long
Trabajador (a)	Hard working
Perezoso (a)	Lazy
Alto (a)	Tall
Bajo (a)	Short (height)
Delgado (a)	Slender
Gordo (a)	Fat
Bonito (a)	Pretty
Guapo (a)	Good looking
Feo (a)	Ugly
Viejo (a)	Old
Nuevo (a)	New
Anciano (a)	Old
Joven	Young
Rápido (a)	Fast
Lento(a)	Slow
Fuerte	Strong
Débil	Weak
Aburrido (a)	Boring

Emocionante	Exciting
Divertido	Fun
Agradable	Nice, pleasant
desagradable	Unpleasant
Cómico (a)	Funny
triste	Sad

Práctica 6.2
Translate the following sentences to Spanish.

1. She is tall. _____

2. He is handsome. _____

3. We are hard working. _____

4. The book is long. _____

5. The movie is short. _____

6. I am short. _____

7. The dogs are fat. _____

8. The blouses are pretty. _____

9. The girls are young. _____

10. The new jackets are ugly.

_____

Práctica 6.3
Read the following story and answer the questions that follow.

En mi ciudad hay un perro pequeño que se llama Buster. Buster es un perro blanco. Buster no es un perro bonito. Es un perro muy feo. También es un perro muy perezoso, pero a Buster le encanta caminar a casas diferentes para comer. Por eso, no es un perro delgado; es un perro muy gordo. Es un perro muy inteligente, y a las familias les gusta mucho porque es un perro muy agradable.

1. ¿Cómo se llama el perro? ¿Buster o Fifí?

2. ¿Es el perro perezoso o energético?

3. ¿De qué color es el perro? ¿Es amarillo o blanco?

4. ¿Es un perro inteligente o estúpido?

5. ¿A las familias les gusta o no les gusta el perro?

Práctica 6.4
Match the following items with a descriptive word. There is no right or wrong answer!
Compare your answers with your partner's.

1. el trabajo   1. _____

2. la playa   2. _____

3. la clase de español   3. _____

4. tus zapatos   4. _____

5. California   5. _____

6. las películas clásicas   6. _____

7. los estudiantes de la clase   7. _____

Chapter 7: Mi Casa Es Tu Casa
Expressing Posession

* Possessive adjectives describe who owns an object. In English they are "my", "your", "his", "hers", "its", "ours" and "theirs".

*Remember adjectives in Spanish agree (match feminine/masculine and singular/plural) with the noun they modify so these possessive adjectives must also agree in gender and number with the noun they are describing!

A. Mi, mis, tu, tus
* To say "**my**" in Spanish use "**mi**" (if the object is singular) or "**mis**" (if the object is plural)

Ejemplo:

Mi libro *(my book)*   Mis libros *(my books)*
Mi hermano *(my brother)*   Mis hermanos *(my brothers)*

* To say "**your**" (when you are talking to a person with whom you are familiar in Spanish use "**tu**" (if the object is singular) or "**tus**" (if the object is plural)

Ejemplo:

Tu libro *(your book)*   Tus libros *(your books)*
Tu hermano *(your brother)*   Tus hermanos *(your brothers)*

B. Su, sus
*To say "**his**", "**her**" or "**your**" (formal) in Spanish use "**su**" (if the object is singular) or "**sus**" (if the object is plural). Notice that "su", then, can refer to lots of different people. Most of the time you will know who you are talking about by the context of the sentence.
Ejemplo:
Su libro *(his book, her book, their book or your book)*
Sus libros *(his books, her books etc.)*

*Sometimes it is necessary to use "**de**" to clarify who the owner is. We do not use the apostrophe in Spanish to show possession. The following are the two ways to show possession:

Ejemplo:
Es el libro de ella. OR Es su libro. *(It is **her** book.)*
Es el libro de ellos. OR Es su libro. *(It is **their** book.)*

C. Nuestro, nuestra, nuestros, nuestras
*To say "**our**" in Spanish use "**nuestro**" or "**nuestra**" (for masculine or feminine and singular nouns) or "**nuestros**" or "**nuestras**" (for masculine or feminine and plural nouns)

Ejemplo:

Nuestro hermano *(our brother)*   Nuestros hermanos *(our brothers)*

Nuestra hermana *(our sister)*   Nuestras hermanas *(our sisters)*

D. Vuestro, vuestra, vuestros, vuestras

*To say "**your**" (plural and familiar… in Spain) in Spanish use "**vuestro**" or "**vuestra**" (for masculine or feminine and singular nouns) or "**vuestros**" or "**vuestras**" (for masculine or feminine and plural nouns)

Ejemplo:

Vuestro hermano *(your brother)*   Vuestros hermanos *(your brothers)*

Vuestra hermana *(your sister)*   Vuestras hermanas *(your sisters)*

Here is a simplified chart of these possessive adjectives:

mi, mis *(my)*	nuestro, nuestra, nuestros, nuestras *(our)*
tu, tus *(your)*	vuestro, vuestra, vuestros, vuestras *(your -informal)*
su, sus *(his, her, its)* *(your- formal)*	su, sus *(their)* *(your – formal)*

Práctica 7.1

Fill-in the blank with the correct possessive adjective according to the sentence.

1. Es (her) _____ prima.

2. Yo preparo (my) _____ proyecto antes de ir al trabajo.

3. Son (their) _____ libros.

4. Es (your, informal, singular) _____ leche.

5. Ellos son (her)_____ sobrinos de Nueva York.

6. (Our) _____ tíos son de México.

7. (Their)_____ camisas son rojas.

8. (Your, plural, informal)_____ botas son grandes.

9. (His) _____ zapatos son negros.

10. Estos son (my) _____ hojas de papel.

11. Es (our) _____ motocicleta.

12. Ella no es (his) _____ hermana.

13. Son (your, informal, singular) _____ perros.

14. La mujer bonita es (their) _____ mamá.

15. (Our) _____ jugo de naranja está aquí.

Dialogues

Diálogo 7.1
Decide which partner will read the part for Estudiante A and who will read Estudiante B. Read the dialogue aloud.

Estudiante A – Hola (partner's first name). ¿Qué tal?

Estudiante B – Estoy muy bien, gracias. ¿Y tú?

Estudiante A – Estoy fantástico(a). Oye, Me gustan mucho las películas de horror. ¿Te gustan también?

Estudiante B – Pues, sí... más or menos, sí.

Estudiante A - ¡Perfecto! Hay una película fenomenal en el cine el viernes. ¿Quieres acompañarme?

Estudiante B - ¡Sí! ¡Cómo no!

Estudiante A - ¡Qué bueno! Nos vemos el viernes.

Estudiante B – Hasta luego.

Diálogo 7.2
Decide which partner will read the part for Estudiante A and who will read Estudiante B. Read the dialogue aloud.

Estudiante A – Hola. ¿Cómo te llamas?

Estudiante B – Me llamo (your name). ¿Y tú?

Estudiante A – Soy (your name). ¿Qué te gusta hacer?

Estudiante B – Me gusta mucho andar en bicicleta por las montañas y también me gusta jugar al tenis.

Estudiante A - ¡Qué interesante! Me gusta andar en bicicleta también, pero no me gusta mucho el tenis. Soy un(a) tenista terrible.

Estudiante B – Ah, sí... pero eres una persona muy activa, ¿no? ¿Qué te gusta hacer en tu tiempo libre?

Estudiante A – Bueno, me gusta ir de compras en la tienda Nordstrom y me gusta pasar tiempo con amigos. También me gusta hacer ejercicio en el gimnasio.

Estudiante B – ¿Te gustan los museos?

Estudiante A – Ah, sí, ¡me encantan!

Estudiante B - ¿Quieres acompañarme al museo esta noche? Es un museo de arte moderno.

Estudiante A – Lo siento, pero no puedo. Tengo que trabajar esta noche. Quizás otro día.

Estudiante B – Muy bien. Quizás el sábado.

Estudiante A – ¿El sábado? Sí, excelente. ¿Nos vemos entonces?

Estudiante B – Sí, hasta luego, (your partner's name).

Diálogo 7.3
Decide which partner will read the part for Estudiante A and who will read Estudiante B. Read the dialogue aloud.

Estudiante A – Buenos días, Sr./Sra. (your partner's last name). ¿Cómo está Ud.?

Estudiante B – Buenos días (your partner's first name). Estoy muy bien, gracias. ¿Cómo estás tú?

Estudiante A – Estoy bien, Sr./Sra. (your partner's last name). Gracias. Sr./Sra. (your partner's last name), ¿A Ud., qué le gusta hacer en su tiempo libre?

Estudiante B – Bueno, (your partner's first name), me gustan muchas actividades. Me gusta leer y practicar deportes. Me gusta usar la computadora y escribir.

Estudiante A - ¿Qué deportes le gustan más?

Estudiante B – A ver… me gusta más el fútbol americano y el baloncesto.

Estudiante A - ¿Y qué le gusta escribir?

Estudiante B – Me gusta escribir poemas románticos.

Estudiante A - ¿Poemas románticos? ¡Qué bueno! ¿Es Ud. muy romántico(a)?

Estudiante B – No, no soy muy romántico(a), pero me gustan mucho las comidas deliciosas.

Estudiante A - ¿Las comidas deliciosas?

Estudiante B – Sí, me gusta escribir poemas para mi esposo(a), y a él/ella le gustan mis poemas románticos. Cuando recibe mi poema romántico, me prepara una comida deliciosa.

Diálogo 7.4
Decide which partner will read the part for Estudiante A and who will read Estudiante B. Read the dialogue aloud.

Estudiante A – Hola, (your partner's name).

Estudiante B – Hola, (your partner's name). ¿Qué tal?

Estudiante A – Bien, gracias. Oye, (your partner's name), ¿qué es esto?

Estudiante B – Es un edificio. Es mi apartamento.

Estudiante A - ¿Tu apartamento? El edificio es muy grande, ¿no?

Estudiante B – Sí, pero mi apartamento es muy pequeño.

Estudiante A – Y, ¿quién es la mujer?

Estudiante B – La mujer es mi hermana, Julia.

Estudiante A – Me gustan sus pantalones morados.

Estudiante B - ¿Sí? A mí no me gustan. Son feos.

Estudiante A - ¿Quién es el hombre con ella?

Estudiante B – El hombre es mi papá.

Estudiante A – Ah. Él es muy alto y delgado. También es muy joven, ¿no?

Estudiante B – Sí, es joven.

Estudiante A - ¿Y el perro? ¿Es tu perro?

Estudiante B – No, no es mi perro. Es el perro de mi hermana. Es muy gordo y
perezoso el perro. No me gusta.

Estudiante A - ¿No te gustan los animales?

Estudiante B – Sí, generalmente me gustan los animales, pero su perro no es mi
favorito. Además, me gustan más los gatos. Son más tranquilos. Los
perros son muy activos.

Estudiante A – A mí me gustan más los perros.

Estudiante B – Bueno, cada cual tiene su propio gusto.

Estudiante A – Sí, es cierto, amigo(a)… es cierto. Bueno, nos vemos pronto, ¿eh?

Estudiante B – Sí, (partner's first name). Chao.

Diálogo 7.5
Decide which partner will read the part for Estudiante A and who will read Estudiante B.
Read the dialogue aloud.

Estudiante A – Hola, (partner's first name). Me gusta tu camisa (add color of shirt your
partner is wearing) ¿Es nueva?

Estudiante B – Sí, es nueva. Muchas gracias.

Estudiante A – Y me gusta(n) mucho tu(s) (choose another item of clothing your partner
is wearing and add a descriptive word). ¿Es/Son nuevo(a,os,as)
también?

Estudiante B – ¡Ay, no! Es/Son muy viejo(a, os, as).

Estudiante A – ¿De qué color son tus ojos? ¿Verdes?

Estudiante B – Mis ojos son (color to match your eyes).

Estudiante A – Tu camisa queda bonita con tus ojos.

Estudiante B – Muchas gracias, (partner's first name).

Estudiante A – De nada.

Diálogo 7.6
Decide which partner will read the part for Estudiante A and who will read Estudiante B.
Read the dialogue aloud.

Estudiante A – Buenos días, Señor/Señora. ¿Me puede ayudar?

Estudiante B – Sí, claro.

Estudiante A – Necesito un suéter nuevo.

Estudiante B - ¿ De qué color?

Estudiante A – Un suéter marrón o negro.

Estudiante B – En el departamento de mujeres, hay suéteres muy bonitos.
Estudiante A – Gracias.
Estudiante B – No hay de que.

Chapter 8: Uno, Dos, Tres...
Numbers in Spanish (And the Word "Hay")

Cero	0			
uno	1			
dos	2		veinte	20
tres	3		treinta	30
cuatro	4		cuarenta	40
cinco	5		cincuenta	50
seis	6		sesenta	60
siete	7		setenta	70
ocho	8		ochenta	80
nueve	9		noventa	90
diez	10		cien (to)	100
Once	11		ciento uno	101
Doce	12		ciento dos	102
Trece	13		ciento trece	113
Catorce	14		doscientos	200
Quince	15		trescientos	300
Dieciséis	16		cuatrocientos	400
Diecisiete	17		quinientos	500
Dieciocho	18		seiscientos	600
Diecinueve	19		setecientos	700
Veinte	20		ochocientos	800
Veintiuno	21		novecientos	900
Veintidós	22		mil	1,000
Veintitrés	23		dos mil	2,000
Veinticuatro	24		doscientos mil	200,000
Veinticinco	25		un millón	1,000,000
Veintiséis	26		dos millones	2,000,000
Veintisiete	27			
Veintiocho	28			
Veintinueve	29			
Treinta	30			
Treinta y uno	31			
Treinta y dos	32			
Treinta y tres	33			
Treinta y cuatro	34			
Treinta y cinco	35			

* In Spanish, the period and comma are reversed: the comma is used for money, and the period is used to show the number.

Ejemplo: (*español*) $2,00 = (*inglés*) $2.00

Ejemplo: (*español*) 2.000.000 = (*inglés*) 2,000,000

Useful Expressions/Questions With Numbers

Hay	There is, there are
¿Cuánto?	How much?
¿Cuánto cuesta?	How much does (it) cost?
¿Cuánto cuestan?	How much do (they) cost?
¿Cuántos (as)?	How many?

Práctica 8.1
Say these numbers aloud and write the numeral that corresponds:

1. seiscientos cuarenta y uno = _____

2. quinientos treinta y cuatro = _____

3. siete mil doscientos once = _____

4. tres milliones setecientos catorce = _____

5. once mil cuatrocientos quince = _____

6. novecientos mil trescientos cincuenta y tres = _____

Práctica 8.2
Answer the following with the number written out in words:

1. ¿Cuánto cuesta este libro? ($15)

   El libro cuesta _____ dólares

2. Cuántos estudiantes hay en la clase? (27)

   Hay _____ estudiantes en la clase.

3. ¿Cuántos relojes (clocks) hay en la clase? (1)

   Hay_____ reloj en la clase.

Práctica 8.3
Write the numbers as a word.

1. 455 _____

2. 49_____

3. 87_____

4. 2,361_____

5. 6,702_____

6. 815_____

7. 9,611 _____

8. 1,213 _____

9. 123 _____

10. 597_____

Práctica 8. 4
Have your partner say a number to you. Write the number in the space provided.

1. _____   6. _____

2. _____   7. _____

3. _____   8. _____

4. _____   9. _____

5. _____   10. _____

Práctica 8.5
Write three years that are important to you in the boxes below. Read them to your partner. Note that we do not read years in Spanish as we do in English. We would not say "nineteen ninety five" for 1995; in Spanish we read the full number, as in: "mil novecientos noventa y cinco".

Year (in number)	Year written

Chapter 9: Mañana Time! Better Late Than Never! Telling Day, Date and Time

Los Días de la Semana ~ The Days of the Week

lunes	Monday
martes	Tuesday
miércoles	Wednesday
jueves	Thursday
viernes	Friday
sábado	Saturday
domingo	Sunday

Useful expressions with the days

Hoy es	Today is
Mañana es	Tomorrow is
Ayer fue	Yesterday was
Anteayer fue	The day before yesterday was
¿Qué día es hoy?	What day is today?
¿Qué día es mañana?	What day is tomorrow?
¿Qué día fue ayer?	What day was yesterday?
¿Qué día de la semana es hoy?	What day of the week is it today?
Si hoy es	If today is....
Si mañana es	If tomorrow is...
Si ayer fue	If yesterday was...

Práctica 9.1
Answer the following questions. Try to answer in complete sentences.

1. ¿Qué día es hoy? _____

2. Si hoy es martes, ¿qué día es mañana?_____

3. Si ayer fue domingo, ¿qué día es hoy? _____

4. Hoy es viernes. ¿Qué día fue ayer? _____

5. ¿Cuál es tu día favorito de la semana? _____

Los meses ~ The months

enero		January
febrero		February
marzo		March
abril		April
mayo		May
junio		June
julio		July
agosto		August
septiembre		September
octubre		October
noviembre		November
diciembre		December

*Note: Days of the week and months of the year are NOT capitalized in Spanish. Use lower case!

Useful expressions with the months

¿En qué mes estamos?	What month is it?
Estamos en (el mes de) ….	It's (the month of) ….
El invierno	the winter
La primavera	The spring
El verano	The summer
El otoño	The fall

Práctica 9.2
Answer the following questions about the months of the year.

1. ¿En qué mes es tu cumpleaños? _____

2. ¿En qué mes es el Día de Acción de Gracias?_____

3. ¿En qué mes es el Día de San Patricio? _____

4. ¿En qué mes es la independencia de Los Estados Unidos?_____

5. ¿En qué mes es el primer día del verano?_____

6. ¿En qué mes es el día de los inocentes? _____

7. ¿En qué mes es la Navidad? _____

8. ¿En qué mes es el Día de San Valentín? _____

9. ¿En qué mes es el primer día del año? _____

10. ¿En qué meses generalmente empiezan las clases de las escuelas?

_____

La Fecha ~ The Date

*To ask what the date is:

¿Cuál es la fecha de hoy?	What is the date today?

*To state the date:
  (Hoy) es el + (the number) + de + (the month)

(Hoy) es el cuatro de julio.	(Today) is the 4th of July (Today) is July 4th.
(Hoy) es el 5 de octubre.	(Today) is the 5th of October. (Today) is October 5th.
Es el dieciséis de septiembre.	It's the 16th of September. It's September 16.

*If it is the first of the month:
  (Hoy) es el primero + de + (the month)

(Hoy) es el primero de febrero.	(Today) is the first of Februrary. (Today) is February first.
Es el primero de diciembre.	It's the first of December. It's December first.

*To state the date with the year:
  Es el + (the number) + de + (the month) + de + (year)

Es el veintiuno de enero de dos mil siete	It's January 21, 2007
Es el once de marzo de mil novecientos noventa y ocho.	It's March 11, 1998.

*To state the day, date, and year together:
  Es (day), + el + (the number) + de + (the month) + de + (year)

Es lunes, el ocho de septiembre de dos mil siete.	It's Monday, September 8, 2007
Es jueves, el 23 de noviembre de dos mil doce.	It's Thursday, November 23, 2012.

*To ask a birthdate:

¿Cuándo es tu cumpleaños?	When is your (informal) birthday?
¿Cuándo es su cumpleaños?	When is your (formal) birthday?
¿Cuándo es el cumpleaños de (tu hermano)?	When is (your brother's) birthday?

*To state a birthdate:
  Es el + (the number) + de + (the month) + de + (year)

Es el diez de febrero de mil novecientos sesenta y nueve.	It's February 10, 1969.
El cumpleaños de mi hermano es el 2 de julio.	My brother's birthday is July 2.
Su cumpleaños es el 11 de mayo.	His/her birthday is May 11.

Práctica 9.3
Talk to three different people and ask them their date of birth. Then record the answer below. Special NOTE: You don't have to include the year on this exercise ☺

Ejemplo:
-¿Cuando es tu cumpleaños?
-Mi cumpleaños es el diez de febrero.
You write: El cumpleaños de _____ es el 10 de febrero. Or Su cumpleaños es el (#) de (month)

1._____

2._____

3._____

La hora ~ The Time

*To tell time in Spanish, we must consider that there is an "academic" way of telling time and an informal way of telling time. The academic way is what you would use in a more formal setting, but is one that is accepted anywhere. The informal way is purely conversational and would be used in casual settings and in places where English has influenced the Spanish being used by the people.

*The academic Spanish involves rounding up to the next hour after you reach the 30 minute marker. In other words, instead of saying, "It's 5:45", you would say, "It's a quarter to 6." Instead of saying, "It's 12:50", you would say, "It's 10 minutes til 1:00".

*The informal method works just like English. If it's 12:50, we say "It's 12 and 50 minutes".

Ejemplos:
1. *It's 1:00* = Es la una
2. *It's 1:15* – Es la una y cuarto
3. *It's 1:30* = Es la una y media
4. *It's 1:45* = Son las dos menos cuarto
5. *It's 2:00* = Son las dos
6. *It's 5:00* = Son las cinco
7. *It's 5:20* = Son las cinco y veinte
8. *It's 5:50* = Son las seis menos diez
9. *It's 12:10* = Son las doce y diez
10. *It's 3:42* = Son las cuatro menos diez y ocho

Expressions With Telling Time

What time is it?	¿Qué hora es?
It is ... o'clock	Es la (when the hour is one) Son las (when the hour is not one)
Quarter past	Y cuarto
Quarter till	Menos cuarto
Thirty	Y media
A.M.	De la mañana
P.M. (from 12 -6)	De la tarde
P.M. (from 6 until 12)	De la noche
It's midnight	Es medianoche
It's noon	Es mediodía
At what time is ...	¿A qué hora es ... ?
It's at ...	Es a la(s) ...
Sharp	En punto
In the (morning(s)/afternoon(s)/evening(s))	Por la(s) (mañana(s), tarde(s), noche(s))

Práctica 9.4
Write the following times in Spanish:

1. It is 4:00 = _____

2. It is 10:15 = _____

3. It is 6:30 = _____

4. It is 2:55 = _____

5. It is 9:35 = _____

6. It is 9:16 = _____

7. It is 12:50 = _____

8. It is 1:10 = _____

9. It is 3:25 = _____

10. It is 5:56 = _____

11. It's noon. = _____

12. It's 5:00 AM = _____

*To ask someone "At what time" something occurs
¿A qué hora (verb)+ (the activity or event)?

¿A qué hora es la fiesta?	At what time is the party?
¿A qué hora empieza la película?	At what time does the movie start?
¿A qué hora llega el tren?	At what time does the train arrive?
¿A qué hora abre el museo?	At what time does the museum open?

*To answer at what time (something happens)
(The activity or event) + (verb) a la(s) + (the time)

La fiesta es a la una.	The party is at 1:00.
La película empieza a las tres.	The movie begins at 3:00.
El tren llega a las cuatro y media.	The train arrives at 4:30.
El museo abre a las ocho.	The museum opens at 8:00.

Práctica 9.5
Answer the following in Spanish.

1. ¿A qué hora llega el autobús? (1:15) _____

_____

2. ¿A qué hora es la fiesta? (8:00 PM) = _____

_____

3. ¿A qué hora empieza (begins) la película? (10:00 sharp)_____

_____

4. ¿A qué hora abre (opens) el museo? (9:30 AM) _____

_____

5. ¿A qué hora sale (leaves) el tren? (2:45 PM) _____

_____

Práctica 9.6
Translate the following sentences to Spanish.

1. The party (la fiesta) is at 11:00

_____

2. The class (La clase) is at 12:45

_____

3. The train arrives (El tren llega) at 6:50

_____

4. The restaurant opens (El restaurante abre) at 8:25

_____

5. The show (La función) is at 5:15

_____

Diálogos

Diálogo 9.1
Read the following dialogue between a professor and a student.

Estudiante: Profesor(a), disculpe, pero ¿cuál es la fecha de hoy?
Profesor(a): Hoy es el catorce de febrero.
Estudiante: ¿El catorce de febrero? ¡No me digas!
Profesor(a): ¿Por qué dices eso?
Estudiante: El catorce de febrero es el Día de San Valentín, ¿no?
Profesor(a): Ah, sí … eso es. ¿Es un día importante para ti?
Estudiante: No, pero es un día importante para Ud.
Profesor(a): ¿Por qué dices eso?
Estudiante: Porque su esposo(a) está allí en la puerta con flores para Ud.

Diálogo 9.2
Read the following dialogue between a husband and wife.

Esposo: ¡Feliz aniversario, querida mía!
Esposa: Gracias, mi amor. Yo también creo que cada día es un aniversario para
          nosotros.
Esposo: Tengo una sorpresa para ti. A las seis, esta noche, para celebrar nuestro
          aniversario, vamos a comer en "Casa Lujosa" – el restaurante más elegante
          del centro de la ciudad. Tengo reservaciones para nosotros dos.

Esposa: ¿En serio? ¿En Casa Lujosa? Pero ese restaurante cuesta un ojo de la cara. Y no es …

Esposo: Pues, así es mi querida. Solo lo mejor para ti. Y eso no es todo. A las ocho, vamos al musical nuevo en el teatro. Tengo asientos reservados. ¡Es fantástico! ¿No crees?

Esposa: Sí, mi amor, pero …

Esposo: No hay peros que valen. Así vamos a celebrar.

Esposa: Bueno, mi amor… pero, ¿cuándo es nuestro aniversario?

Esposo: ¡Es hoy!

Esposa: ¿Cuál es la fecha de hoy?

Esposo: Es el doce de julio, ¿no?

Esposa: Sí, mi amor. Es el doce de julio. Pero nuestro aniversario es el doce de agosto.

Esposo: ¡Ay, caramba!

Esposa: No te preocupes, mi amor. No hay problema. Celebramos nuestro aniversario con una cena elegante y un musical nuevo el doce de julio Y el doce de agosto. ¡Qué buena idea! ¿No crees?

Chapter 10: Weather or Not, Here We Come!
Describing the weather

Expressions Involving Weather

El tiempo	The weather
¿Qué tiempo hace?	What's the weather like?
¿Qué tiempo hace afuera hoy?	What's the weather outside today?
¿Qué tiempo hace en enero?	What's the weather like in January?
¿Qué tiempo hace en su/tu pueblo/ciudad?	What's the weather like in your town/city?
Las estaciones	The seasons
¿En qué estación estamos?	What's the season?
El verano	The summer
El invierno	The winter
El otoño	The fall
La primavera	The spring
Estamos en (season)... Estamos en otoño	It's (the season)... It's fall
Hace buen tiempo.	It's nice weather
Hace mal tiempo.	It's bad weather.
Hace sol.	It's sunny.
Hace calor.	It's hot.
Hace frío.	It's cold.
Hace fresco.	It's cool/chilly.
Hace viento.	It's windy.
Hace (75) grados.	It's (75) degrees.
Está húmedo.	It's humid.
Está nublado.	It's cloudy.
Hay granizo.	There's hail.
Nieva.	Its' snowing.
Llueve.	It's raining.
Llueve a cántaros.	It's raining cats and dogs.
La nieve.	The snow

La lluvia	The rain
La niebla	The fog.
La tormenta	The storm
¡Qué frío/calor/húmedo/viento!	It's so cold/hot/humid/windy!

Clothing Items

La ropa	The clothing
La camisa	The shirt
La camiseta	The t-shirt
El abrigo	The coat
Los pantalones	The pants
La bufanda	The scarf
Los guantes	The gloves
La gorra	The cap/hat
El suéter	The sweater
El impermeable	The raincoat
El paraguas	The umbrella
Los shorts / pantalones cortos	The shorts
Los zapatos	The shoes
Las sandalias	The sandals
Las botas	The boots
Los tacones	The heels
El traje de baño	The bathing suit
La blusa	The blouse
El vestido	The dress
La chaqueta	The jacket
El conjunto	The outfit
La falda	The skirt
El calcetín (Los calcetines)	The sock (the socks)
La casaca	The sports jacket
El traje	The suit
Las medias	The tights/pantyhose
La ropa interior	The underwear
El chaleco	The vest
El cinturón / la correa	The belt
La pulsera	The bracelet
Los aretes	The earrings
Las gafas / los lentes	The glasses
La bolsa	The handbag
El collar	The necklace
El anillo	The ring
El pañuelo	The handkerchief
Las gafas de sol	The sunglasses
La corbata	The tie

Los cordones	The shoelaces
El botón	The button
El bolsillo	The pocket
El cuello	The collar
La manga	The sleeve
El cierre	The zipper
La pana	The corduroy
El algodón	The cotton
El cuero	The leather
El lino	The linen
La seda	The silk
La lana	The wool
La tela	The fabric
La marca	The brand
La talla	The size (clothing)
El número	The size (shoes)

Práctica 10.1
Answer the following questions in complete sentences.

1. ¿Qué tiempo hace en otoño? _____

2. ¿Llueve mucho en abril? _____

3. ¿Te gusta la lluvia? _____

4. ¿Nieva aquí en nuestra ciudad? _____

5. ¿Qué tiempo hace en California? _____

6. ¿Qué te gusta llevar (to wear) en el invierno?

_____

7. ¿Lleva un suéter o un traje de baño cuando hace frío?

_____

8. ¿Lleva un suéter o una camiseta cuando hace fresco?

_____

9. ¿Lleva una bufanda o una camiseta cuando hace calor?

_____

10. ¿Lleva un impermeable cuando llueve?

Práctica 10.2
Choose one partner to read the story and ask the questions in parentheses. The other partner will listen to the story and answer the questions. The translation to the story and the answers to the questions are in the appendix if you need them!

Hay una mujer que se llama Marisol. *(¿Cómo se llama la mujer – Marta o Marisol?)* **Marisol va a ir a una fiesta esta noche a las ocho.** *(¿Adónde va Marisol – a una clase o a una fiesta?)* **Marisol está muy emocionada porque le gustan las fiestas.** *(¿Está Marisol enojada o emocionada?)* *(¿A Marisol le gustan o no le gustan las fiestas?)* **También está emocionada porque le gusta mucho un hombre que se llama Diego y Diego va a estar en la fiesta también.** *(¿A Marisol le gusta o no le gusta Diego?)* *(¿Va a estar en la fiesta Diego – sí o no?)* **Pero Marisol tiene un problema. No sabe qué llevar a la fiesta.** *(¿Qué problema tiene Marisol – no tiene dinero o no sabe qué llevar?)* **Hace mucho frío pero no desea llevar un suéter y pantalones. Prefiere llevar un vestido corto sin mangas.** *(¿Prefiere Marisol llevar unos pantalones o un vestido?)* **Pero nieva y hace mucho frío.** *(¿Hace calor o hace frío?)* **Decide llevar un vestido corto y rojo con un suéter y unos tacones.** *(¿Decide llevar los pantalones o el vestido?)*

Marisol llega a la fiesta a las ocho y media. *(¿Llega Marisol a tiempo a la fiesta o un poco tarde?)* **Marisol ve a Diego inmediatamente. Diego lleva unos jeans, botas, y un abrigo. Todos en la fiesta llevan ropa para el invierno.** *(¿Llevan las personas la ropa para el invierno o para el verano?)* **Hay otra persona que lleva un vestido corto también. Es una mujer alta con el pelo largo y castaño.** *(¿Lleva la mujer alta los pantalones o un vestido?)* **La mujer llega al lado de Diego y le da un beso. Marisol se da cuenta de que Diego tiene novia.** *(¿Tiene novia Diego – sí o no?)* *(¿Es Marisol la novia de Diego – sí o no?)* **En este momento, Marisol tiene frío y quiere sus pantalones y su suéter.** *(¿Está contenta Marisol en su vestido?)*

Chapter 11: Whatcha Doin'?
Saying What People Do (Using Verbs)

* **There are three types of verbs in Spanish:**

  1. Verbs ending in - **AR**

  2. Verbs ending in - **ER**

  3. Verbs ending in - **IR**

*If we want to express that an action takes place in the present time, we must CONJUGATE or CHANGE the ENDING of the verb to match the SUBJECT of the sentence. The endings we use are determined according to the SUBJECT and the TYPE of ending the verb has.

*When the ending of the verb has not been conjugated (changed) it is called the INFINITIVE.

How to conjuage regular –AR verbs:

- **Stems**
  In order to CONJUGATE (or change) a verb in Spanish you must first form the **STEM** of the verb. To form the STEM, first drop the –AR ending off of the infinitive.

Práctica 11.1
Write the stem of each verb by dropping off the ending.

Infinitive	English	Stem
hablar	to speak, to talk	*habl*
ayudar a	to help	
buscar	to search, look for	
contestar	to answer	
desear	to desire, to want	

Verb Endings for –AR Verbs

After you form the stem by dropping the –AR ending, add these new endings to END the verb stem.

Yo	- o	Nosotros Nosotras	- amos
Tú	- as	Vosotros Vosotras	- áis
Él Ella Usted	- a	Ellos Ellas Ustedes	- an

Ejemplo: **LLevar-to wear**

Yo	**llevo**	Nosotros Nosotras	**llevamos**
Tú	**llevas**	Vosotros Vosotras	**lleváis**
Él Ella Usted	**lleva**	Ellos Ellas Ustedes	**llevan**

Práctica 11.2

Conjugate the verb "estudiar" to the present tense.

Estudiar-to study

Yo		Nosotros Nosotras	
Tú		Vosotros Vosotras	
Él Ella Usted		Ellos Ellas Ustedes	

List of Common Regular – AR Verbs:

Andar	To walk, to ride, to go around
Arreglar	To fix, to arrange
Ayudar	To help
Bailar	To dance
Buscar	To look for
Caminar	To walk
Cantar	To sing
Cenar	To eat dinner
Charlar	To chat
Chismear	To gossip
Comprar	To buy
Contestar	To answer
Descansar	To rest
Desear	To desire, to want
Enseñar	To teach, to show
Entrar (en)	To enter (in)
Escuchar	To listen to
Esperar	To wait, to hope for
Estudiar	To study
Hablar	To speak, to talk
Lavar	To wash
Limpiar	To clean
Llamar	To call
Llegar	To arrive
Llevar	To wear
Mandar	To send
Mirar	To watch
Nadar	To swim
Necesitar	To need
Organizar	To organize

Participar	To participate
Pasar	To spend (time), to happen, to pass
Patinar	To skate
Preparar	To prepare
Sacar, (sacar fotos)	To take out, (to take photos)
Tocar	To touch, to play (an instrument)
Tomar	To take, to drink
Trabajar	To work
Usar	To use
Viajar	To travel

Práctica 11.3

Write the correct form of the verb in parenthesis. Change the verb to match the subject.

1. La muchacha _____(hablar) con los amigos.

2. Los estudiantes _____(sacar) los libros de las mochilas.

3. ¿ _____(llegar) vosotros en autobús?

4. Carlos y yo _____(llevar) trajes al trabajo.

5. La profesora _____(enseñar) la lección.

6. David y Juan _____(tomar) una clase de español.

7. Ustedes siempre _____(estudiar) mucho.

8. ¿ _____(mirar) tú mucha televisión?

9. Yo _____(escuchar) la radio en la tarde.

10. Los estudiantes _____(entrar) en la sala de clase a las siete en punto.

11. María y tú _____(estudiar) para la clase de español.

12. Los alumnos buenos _____(escuchar) a la profesora. ☺

13. Los alumnos malos no_____(participar) en la clase. ☺

14. Yo siempre _____(llevar) un bolígrafo y unas hojas de papel en mi mochila.

15. Muchos de mis amigos _____(pasar) las vacaciones en las montañas.

Práctica 11.4

Translate the following sentences to Spanish.
NOTE: To make a statement, the subject goes first and the verb after. If you are asking a question, the verb comes before the subject.

1. I need a pencil. _____

2. She wants some books. _____

3. We speak Spanish! _____

4. They chat with their friends. _____

5. Do you (inf.) listen to the music? _____

Práctica 11.5

Answer the questions in complete sentences about yourself. Then, ask your partner the same questions and compare your answers.

1. ¿Hablas tú francés o inglés?

_____

2. ¿Ayuda tu esposo(a)?

_____

3. ¿Qué programa miras tú en la televisión?

_____

4. ¿Buscas tú un diccionario?

_____

5. ¿Llevas tú los jeans al trabajo?

_____

6. ¿Pasas tú mucho tiempo con tu familia?

_____

Diálogos

Diálogo 11.1

Choose a role – Carla or Marta. Then read the dialogue aloud with your partner. Pay attention to the changing of the endings for the –AR verbs in the dialogue.

Carla **-** ¿Qué buscas, Marta?

Marta **-** ¿Yo? Busco un lugar interesante para visitar este fin de semana. Mi amigo, Jorge, llega el sábado.

Carla **-** ¿Qué deseas hacer?

Marta – A Jorge le gustan mucho los museos. Deseo ir a un museo de arte.

Carla – Mi vecino trabaja en el Museo Getty. Él organiza las visitas de los turistas y es un museo muy interesante y bonito.

Marta – Es una idea fantástica, Carla. Llamo a tu vecino hoy. Muchas gracias.

Diálogo 11.2

Choose a role – Susana or Carlos. Then read the dialogue aloud with your partner. Pay attention to the changing of the endings for the –AR verbs in the dialogue.

Susana **-** ¿Qué haces los fines de semana, Carlos?

Carlos – ¿Los fines de semana? Yo estudio mis lecciones de español, hablo con amigos, miro la tele, y a veces bailo por las noches. ¿Y tú, Susana?

Susana – Los viernes ceno con mi familia en un restaurante fabuloso. Los sábados yo charlo con amigos y limpio mi casa.

Carlos **-** ¿Y los domingos?

Susana **-** ¿Los domingos? Después de limpiar mi casa, ¡yo descanso!

How to conjugate regular "-er" verbs

Práctica 11. 6

Write the stem of each of the following –er verbs by dropping off the ending:
"-er" verbs

Infinitive	English	Stem
comer	To eat	*com*
beber	To drink	
leer	To read	
vender	To sell	

75

Endings for "-er" verbs

After you form the stem add these endings to the stem of the verb.

Yo	- o	Nosotros Nosotras	- emos
Tú	- es	Vosotros Vosotras	- éis
Él Ella Usted	- e	Ellos Ellas Ustedes	- en

Ejemplo:

Comer = to eat

Yo	como	Nosotros Nosotras	comemos
Tú	comes	Vosotros Vosotras	coméis
Él Ella Usted	come	Ellos Ellas Ustedes	comen

Práctica 11.7

Conjugate the verb "leer" to the present tense.

Leer = to read

Yo		Nosotros Nosotras	
Tú		Vosotros Vosotras	
Él Ella Usted		Ellos Ellas Ustedes	

List of Common Regular -ER Verbs

Aprender	To learn
Barrer	To sweep
Beber	To drink
Comer	To eat
Comprender	To understand, comprehend
Correr	To run
Creer	To believe
Deber	Should, ought to (followed by infinitive)
Leer	To read
Vender	To sell

Práctica 11.8
Fill in the blank with the correct form of the verb.

1. Ella (reads/leer) _____ muchos libros románticos.

2. Los estudiantes de español (learn/aprender) _____ mucho en la clase.

3. Yo (believe/creer) _____ que el español es fácil.

4. Tú y yo (run/correr) _____ por las noches.

5. ¿(Do you sell/vender) _____ tú libros viejos aquí?

Práctica 11.9
Answer the following questions about yourself. Then, ask the same questions to your partner. Compare your answers and make sure you are using the correct endings.
Ejemplo:

    Estudiante A   - ¿Lees tú muchos libros cómicos?

    Estudiante B   - Sí, yo leo muchos libros cómicos?

1. ¿Crees tú en los fantasmas (ghosts)?

_____

2. ¿Comes tú en restaurantes caros (expensive)?

_____

3. ¿Come tu familia en restaurantes de comida rápida?

_____

4. ¿Comprenden tus amigos el español?

_____

5. ¿Bebes tú el vino (wine) rojo?

_____

* The irregular verb **"Ver"** means **"to see"**

* "Ver" works like the other –er verbs listed above, except in the "yo" and "tú" forms. In these two forms, the "e" is not dropped to form the stem; instead, the "e" is kept in the conjugation.

Conjugations of the verb "ver" (to see)

(yo)	**veo**	(nosotros)	**vemos**
(tú)	**ves**	(vosotros)	**veis**
(él, ella, Usted)	**ve**	(ellos, ellas, Ustedes) **ven**	

Práctica 11.10
Translate the following sentences using the verb "ver".

1. I see the big dog. = _____

2. Do you see many movies? = _____

How to Conjugate Regular "-ir" verbs

Práctica 11.11
Write the stem of each of the following –ir verbs by dropping off the ending:

"-ir" verbs

Infinitive	English	Stem
vivir	To live	*viv*
abrir	To open	
compartir	To share	
escribir	To write	
recibir	To receive	

Endings for "-ir" verbs

After you form the stem add these endings to stem the verb.

Yo		Nosotros	
	- o	Nosotras	**- imos**
Tú		Vosotros	
	- es	Vosotras	**- ís**
Él		Ellos	
Ella		Ellas	
Usted	**- e**	Ustedes	**- en**

Ejemplo: **Vivir = to live**

Yo		Nosotros	
	vivo	Nosotras	**vivimos**
Tú		Vosotros	
	vives	Vosotras	**vivís**
Él		Ellos	
Ella		Ellas	
Usted	**vive**	Ustedes	**viven**

*Notice the difference between the "-er" and "-ir" endings. All of the endings are the same except the nosotros and the vosotros forms.

Práctica 11.12
Conjugate the verb "vivir" to the present tense:

abrir-to open

Yo	Nosotros
	Nosotras
Tú	Vosotros
	Vosotras
Él	Ellos
Ella	Ellas
Usted	Ustedes

List of Common Regular -IR Verbs

Abrir	To open
Asistir (a)	To attend
Compartir	To share
Cubrir	To cover
Escribir	To write
Recibir	To receive
Subir	To go up, climb
Vivir	To live

Práctica 11.13
Fill in the blank with the correct form of the verb.

1. Nosotros _____(recibir) muchos regalos en nuestros cumpleaños.

2. Juan y tú _____(vivir) en la ciudad de Glendale.

3. Mis padres _____(compartir) el carro.

4. José y Juana _____(subir) las escaleras (the stairs) para llegar al

   tercer piso.

5. Paula _____(escribir) un artículo para el periódico.

6. Ustedes _____(abrir) los libros en la clase de español.

Práctica 11.14
Translate the following questions to Spanish. Then ask your partner the questions you've just translated.

1. Do you write poems (los poemas)?

   _____

2. Do you receive a lot of phone calls (llamadas telefónicas)?

   _____

3. Do you share your house with another person (con otra persona)?

   _____

4. Do you share your car with another person?

_____

5. Do you attend other classes (otras clases)?

_____

REVIEW OF ALL ENDINGS:

-AR VERBS   **-ER VERBS**   **-IR VERBS**

Singular	plural		Singular	plural		singular	plural
-o	**-amos**		**-o**	**-emos**		**-o**	**-imos**
-as	-áis		-es	-éis		-es	-ís
-a	-an		-e	-en		-e	-en

Práctica 11.15
Decide if you are Estudiante A or Estudiante B. Have a conversation with your partner by asking the questions under your column and answering the questions your partner asks you. Note that the type of verb varies (some are –ar, some –er, and some –ir). Pay attention to the change of endings to match both your subject and verb type.

Estudiante A

1. ¿Comprendes esta lección?
2. ¿Charlas con amigos por computadora?
3. ¿Vives en una casa grande o pequeña?
4. ¿Trabajas en una oficina o en tu casa?
5. ¿Aprendes rápidamente o lentamente?

Estudiante B

1. ¿Lees novelas de misterio?
2. ¿Viajas a países diferentes?
3. ¿Asistes a muchas fiestas?
4. ¿Tocas un instrumento?
5. ¿Miras muchas películas?

Diálogos

Diálogo 11.3
Decide with your partner who will read the part of Estudiante A and who will read Estudiante B. Read the dialogue aloud and focus on the change of endings for each verb.

Estudiante A – Hola, amigo(a)….¿qué tal?

Estudiante B – Bien, amigo. Muy bien. ¿Y tú?

Estudiante A – Bien, bien… gracias. Oye, ¿cuál es la fecha de hoy?

Estudiante B – Pues, hoy es el diez y siete de marzo. Es el Día de San Patricio. ¿Por qué?

Estudiante A – No me gusta chismear, pero nuestra amiga – la profesora – bebe cerveza verde ahora.

Estudiante B - ¿De veras? Creo que es para celebrar el Día de San Patricio. ¿No crees?

Estudiante A – Creo que sí, pero también creo que no debemos hablar más de esto. La profesora no debe beber cerveza en la clase.

Estudiante B – Bueno, estoy de acuerdo.

Diálogo 11.4
Decide with your partner who will read the part of Estudiante A and who will read Estudiante B. Read the dialogue aloud and focus on the change of endings for each verb.

Estudiante A – Buenos días, Señor(a). ¿Usa Ud. la computadora aquí?

Estudiante B – Buenos días. Sí, la uso. ¿Desea Ud. usar la computadora?

Estudiante A – Sí, busco información por la red.

Estudiante B – Bueno, termino dentro de unos minutos. ¿Desea Ud. esperar un rato?

Estudiante A – No, no deseo esperar. Busco otra computadora. Gracias.

Estudiante B – De nada.

Diálogo 11.5
Decide with your partner who will read the part of Estudiante A and who will read Estudiante B. Read the dialogue aloud and focus on the change of endings for each verb.

Estudiante A – Hola, Mamá. ¿Qué preparas para la cena?

Estudiante B – Preparo unos tamales con carne y arroz con pollo.

Estudiante A – Fantástico. ¿Y cuándo comemos?

Estudiante B - A las seis en punto, hijo. Debes lavarte las manos ahora mismo.

Estudiante A – Bueno, Mamá. ¿Miramos una película mientras cenamos? Deseo ver un programa en la tele.

Estudiante B – No, mi hijo, no. Hablamos de nuestro día mientras cenamos. No deseamos mirar un programa mientras comemos. No es saludable mirar la tele y comer a la vez.

Estudiante A – Eres la mamá más aburrida de todas.

Estudiante B – Pobrecito… pero así es la vida.

Diálogo 11.6
Decide with your partner who will read the part of Estudiante A and who will read Estudiante B. Read the dialogue aloud and focus on the change of endings for each verb.

Estudiante A – Buenos días, mi querida.

Estudiante B – Buenos días, mi amor.

Estudiante A - ¿Deseas subir una montaña hoy?

Estudiante B - ¿Subir una montaña? No, mi amor. No deseo subir una montaña. ¿Deseas tú ir de compras?

Estudiante A – Claro que no, mi querida. No hay suficiente dinero para ir de compras contigo. ¿Miramos el partido de béisbol entre los Dodgers y los Giants?

Estudiante B – Ay, mi amor. No. Ah, yo sé … ¿patinamos de la mano por la playa?

Estudiante A – Querida mía, no patino bien. Eh, yo sé… ¿nadamos en el agua del océano?

Estudiante B - ¿Yo? ¿Llevar un traje de baño enfrente de todo el mundo? No. Bueno, ¿bailamos al ritmo la música aquí en la casa? ¡Qué romántico! ¿No crees?

Estudiante A – Sí, es muy romántico. Pero… no. No bailo bien tampoco.

Estudiante B – Amor mío, deseo hacer algo hoy. ¿Comemos algo?

Estudiante A – Es una idea fantástica, mi querida. ¿Qué preparas tú para comer?

Práctica 11.16
¿Qué tenemos en común? (What do we have in common?)
Respond to the questions for yourself in the first column by writing "sí" or "no". Then, ask your partner and write his/her responses in the second column. See how much you have in common! ☺

Pregunta	Yo	Mi compañero/a
1. ¿Charlas con tus amigos en clase?		
2. ¿Arreglas los coches?		
3. ¿Llamas a tus amigos por teléfono cada noche?		
4. ¿Bebes mucha leche?		
5. ¿Lees novelas románticas?		
6. ¿Lees novelas de misterio?		
7. ¿Crees en los fantasmas (ghosts)?		
8. ¿Leen mucho tus amigos?		
9. ¿Ves muchas películas en el cine?		
10. ¿Escribes poemas?		
11. ¿Recibes muchas cartas de tu novio/a (boyfriend/girlfriend)?		
12. ¿Asistes a muchas reuniones?		
13. ¿Necesitas mucha atención?		

14. ¿Cenas con tu familia cada noche?		
15. ¿Compras mucha ropa cara?		
16. ¿Lavas los platos después de comer?		
17. ¿Miras mucha televisión?		
18. ¿Usas mucho la computadora?		
19. ¿Estudias en tu cama (bed)?		
20. ¿Deseas vivir en una casa grande?		
21. ¿Vives en un apartamento elegante?		
22. ¿Sacas muchas fotos?		
23. ¿Escuchas música en español?		
24. ¿Escuchas el radio en el coche?		
25. ¿Aprendes rápidamente?		
26. ¿Te gusta subir las montañas?		

Chapter 12: Never Say Never
Showing How Often People Do Activities
(Frequency/Adverbs)

Useful Adverbs

Siempre	Always
Todos los días	Every day
Mucho	Often
A menudo	Often
A veces	Sometimes
De vez en cuando	Once in a while
Poco	A little
Rara vez	Rarely
Nunca	Never
Jamás	Not at all, never ever!
Cada	Each, every

*Generally, the following adverbs go BEFORE the VERB:

1. siempre … Isabel siempre llega tarde a clase.

2. rara vez … Isabel rara vez escucha a la profesora en clase.

3. nunca … Isabel nunca usa un diccionario.

4. jamás … Isabel jamás participa en clase.

*Generally, the following adverbs go AFTER the VERB:

1. mucho … Isabel habla mucho con sus amigos en la clase.

2. poco … Isabel estudia poco para la clase.

*The following longer phrases can go either at the BEGINNING or END of the SENTENCE:

1. todos los días …

    Todos los días Isabel asiste a clase. OR Isabel asiste a clase todos los dias.

2. a veces …

    A veces Isabel descansa en clase. OR Isabel descansa en clase a veces.

3. de vez en cuando…

    De vez en cuando Isabel presta atención en clase. OR Isabel presta atención en clase de vez en cuando.

Práctica 12.1
State how often you do or don't do these activites.

Ejemplo: hablar en francés... *Yo nunca hablo en francés.*

1. mirar la televisión

_____

2. escribir poemas

_____

3. cocinar en casa

_____

4. usar la computadora

_____

5. tomar una clase

_____

6. comprar ropa nueva

_____

7. hablar con tus padres

_____

8. practicar el español

_____

Práctica 12.2
Choose one partner to ask the even questions and the other to ask the odd. Ask your partner and answer with how often you do or don't do these activities.

1. ¿Con qué frecuencia lees el periódico?
2. ¿Con qué frecuencia caminas con tu perro?
3. ¿Con qué frecuencia escuchas música?
4. ¿Con qué frecuencia descansas durante el día?
5. ¿Con qué frecuencia viajas?
6. ¿Con qué frecuencia usas un diccionario?
7. ¿Con qué frecuencia tocas un instrumento?
8. ¿Con qué frecuencia limpias la casa?
9. ¿Con qué frecuencia ves a tus parientes?
10. ¿Con qué frecuencia caminas al supermercado?

Chapter 13: Who? What? When? Where? Why?

Asking Questions (Interrogatives)

* There are many ways to ask questions. The following examples show how you create a simple question that has a yes or no answer.

> <u>Statement</u>: Isabel va a la escuela.
> > <u>Question</u>: ¿Va Isabel a la escuela?
> > <u>Answer</u>: Sí, Isabel va a la escuela (or) No, Isabel no va a la escuela.

*Some questions are formed by putting a conjugated verb after the question word.

> <u>Statement</u>: Isabel va a la escuela.
> > <u>Question</u>: ¿Adónde va Isabel?
> > <u>Answer</u>: Isabel va a la escuela.

Question words (interrogatives) that are generally followed by a verb:

Question Word	Translation	Example
¿cómo?	How? (What is something like?)	Q - ¿Cómo es Arturo? A – Arturo es alto y muy romántico.
¿Cuál? ¿Cuáles?	Which one? Which ones?	Q - ¿Cuál es tu color favorito? A – Mi color favorito es verde. Q - ¿Cuáles son tus deportes favoritos? A – Mis deportes favoritos son el fútbol y el patinaje.
¿Cuándo?	When?	Q - ¿Cuándo llegas a la clase? A – Llego a la clase a las siete de la noche.
¿Cuánto? ¿Cuántos? ¿Cuántas?	How much? How many? (masculine items) How many? (feminine items)	Q - ¿Cuánto cuesta el collar? A – El collar cuesta seis dólares. Q - ¿Cuántos libros hay en la clase? A – Hay treinta libros en la clase. Q - ¿Cuántas camisas hay en la tienda? A – Hay muchas camisas en la tienda.
¿Dónde?	Where?	Q - ¿Dónde está el correo (post office)? A – El correo está al lado del banco.
¿Adónde?	To where?	Q - ¿Adónde vas tú? A – Voy a la clase de español.
¿De dónde?	From where?	Q - ¿De dónde es Ud.? A – Yo soy de Los Estados Unidos.
¿Por qué?	Why?	Q - ¿Por qué lees el libro? A – Leo el libro porque me gusta la historia.
¿Qué?	What?	Q - ¿Qué es esto? A – Es un edificio.
¿Quién? ¿Quiénes?	Who (is)? Who (are)?	Q- ¿Quién es la mujer? A – La mujer es mi mamá. Q - ¿Quiénes son los hombres? A – Los hombres son mis hermanos.

* Sometimes "¿qué?" and "¿Cuál(es)?" are followed by words other than verbs. "¿Qué?" can be followed by a NOUN, but "¿Cuál(es)?" cannot. Use "¿cuál?" for one item and "¿cuáles?" for more than one.

    Example: -¿<u>Qué</u> libro mira Isabel? = What book is Isabel looking at?
                       -¿<u>Cuá</u>les de los libros mira Isabel? = Which books is Isabel looking at?

Práctica 13.1
Think of question words you could use with the following sentences:

Ejemplo:
Mateo es una persona muy tranquila.
Possible questions one could ask about that statement:
¿Cómo es Mateo?... ¿Quién es una persona muy tranquila?

1. Mis padres hablan español.

2. Hay cinco libros en la clase.

3. El libro es un diccionario.

4. Luisa descansa en su cuarto?

5. Yo estudio por la mañana.

6. Jorge es delgado y vive en el apartamento en la calle Monte Vista.

Práctica 13.2
Translate the following questions to Spanish.

1. Where is the park? _____

2. Who is reading the book? _____

3. (To) where are you going? _____

4. How much does the necklace cost? _____

5. How many beds (camas) are there in the room (cuarto)?

    _____

6. Why are you studying Spanish? _____

Diálogo 13.1
Decide which partner will play the role of the child and which will play the role of the parent. Read the dialogue aloud.

Padre/Madre:	Hijo(a), necesitas zapatos. ¿Dónde están?
Hijo(a):	Están en el garaje. Pero, ¿por qué necesito mis zapatos?
Padre/Madre:	Necesitas tus zapatos porque vamos al supermercado.
Hijo(a):	¿Y por qué vamos al supermercado?
Padre/Madre:	Vamos al supermercado porque necesitamos comida.
Hijo(a):	¿Por qué necesitamos comida del supermercado? ¿Por qué no vamos al restaurante para comer?
Padre/Madre:	No vamos al restaurante porque cuesta mucho dinero comprar comida en los restaurantes.
Hijo(a):	¿Por qué cuesta mucho la comida de los restaurantes?
Padre/Madre:	Cuesta mucho dinero porque pagamos por el servicio y por los cocineros que preparan la comida para nosotros.
Hijo(a):	¿Por qué pagamos por el servicio?
Padre/Madre:	Pagamos por el servicio porque … ay, hijo(a)… no sé. Ponte los zapatos y vámonos.

Diálogo 13.2
Decide which partner will play the role of the employer and which will play the role of the applicant. Read the dialogue aloud.

El/La empleador/a:	Buenos días. Siéntese, por favor.
El/La solicitante:	Buenos días. Gracias.
El/La empleador/a:	A Ud. le gustaría trabajar para nosotros. ¿Verdad?
El/La solicitante:	Sí. Me gustaría ser vendedor/a aquí.
El/La empleador/a:	Bueno. Tengo unas preguntas para Ud. Primero, ¿cuál es su dirección?
El/La solicitante:	Vivo en la calle Sierra Vista número 2365 en Los Ángeles, California.
El/La empleador/a:	Bueno. Y, ¿cómo se escribe su apellido?
El/La solicitante:	Mi apellido es Bengoa. Be-e-ene-ge-o-a
El/La empleador/a:	Y, ¿Qué experiencia tiene Ud. en ser vendedor/a?
El/La solicitante:	Hace tres años que soy vendedor/a en la tienda "Joyas". Vendo anillos con diamantes, pulseras de plata, aretes de oro y mucho más. Hay muchas personas a las cuales les gustan las joyas.
El/La empleador/a:	¡Sí, lo creo! Y, ¿cuánto dinero recibe Ud. cada mes por su trabajo ahora?
El/La solicitante:	¡Uf! ¡Mucho! Casi cinco mil dólares cada mes. Es increíble.
El/La empleador/a:	¿Cinco mil dólares? Bueno, Señor/a, no comprendo. ¿Por qué desea Ud. ser vendedor/a aquí? No va a ganar tanto dinero aquí.
El/La solicitante:	¿Por qué? La respuesta es fácil, Señor/a. En la tienda donde trabajo, yo debo trabajar mucho porque hay muchos clientes. Aquí no hay tantos clientes y no voy a trabajar tanto. Es más importante descansar y disfrutar la vida que trabajar. ¿No cree Ud.?

Chapter 14: Whatsa Mattah You?
Expressing How You Feel
(Using the Verbs "Tener", "Estar", and "Sentirse")

* To express how we feel, we generally use the verb "estar" (to be). Here are the conjugations of the verb "estar" in the present tense:

estoy	estamos
estás	estáis
está	están

Here are some feeling words that are used with the verb "estar":

Enojado (a) or enfadado (a)	Angry
Ansioso (a)	Anxious
Apático (a)	Apathetic
Aburrido (a)	Bored
Ocupado (a)	Busy
Cómodo (a) or confortable	Comfortable
Seguro (a) (seguro/a de mí mismo/a, ti mismo/a)	Confident, sure (sure of myself, yourself)
Confuso (a)	Confused
Curioso (a)	Curious
Deprimido (a)	Depressed
Decepcionado (a)	Disappointed
Desanimado (a)	Discouraged
Disgustado (a)	Disgusted, upset
Distraído (a)	Distracted
Avergonzado (a)	Embarrassed
Emocionado (a)	Excited
Harto (a)	Fed up
Feliz	Happy
Optimista or esperanzado (a)	Hopeful
Dolido (a)	Hurt
De mal humor	In a bad mood
De buen humor	In a good mood
Enamorado (a) (de)	In love
Inspirado (a)	Inspired
Aislado (a)	Isolated
Amado (a)	Loved
Travieso (a)	Mischeivous
Nervioso (a)	Nervous
En las nubes	On cloud nine

Pensativo (a)	Pensive
Aliviado (a)	Relieved
Triste	Sad
Satisfecho (a)	Satisfied
Tímido (a)	Shy
Loco (a)	Silly
Estresado (a)	Stressed
Asustado (a)	Surprised
Cansado (a)	Tired
Tranquilo (a)	Tranquil, calm
Preocupado (a)	Worried

Práctica 14.1

Pick three adjectives from above to describe how you feel/how you are right now and write them on the blank lines below. Make sure you use the right ending to match your gender.

1. Estoy _____

2. Estoy _____

3. Estoy _____

Práctica 14.2

Pick three adjectives from above to describe how you <u>don't</u> feel right now and write them on the blank lines below. Make sure you use the right ending to match your gender.

1. No estoy _____

2. No estoy _____

3. No estoy _____

*We also use the verb "sentirse" to express how we feel. Here are the conjugations for the verb "sentirse":

Me siento	Nos sentimos
Te sientes	Os sentís
Se siente	Se sienten

1. *I feel sad.* = Me siento triste.

2. *She feels hurt.* = Ella se siente dolida.

3. *We feel frustrated.* = Nos sentimos frustrados.

Práctica 14.3

Choose one partner to read/ask the odd numbered questions and the other to ask the even numbered ones. Ask your partner the questions, and when you each answer, use the information in parenthesis in your response. Make sure you use the correct ending for the adjective to match your gender.

Ejemplo:

  -¿Estás muy nervioso/a ahora? (No - tranquilo/a)
  - *No, no estoy nervioso/a; estoy tranquilo/a.*

1. ¿Estás muy cansado/a esta noche? (No - preocupado/a).

2. ¿Te sientes muy desanimado/a con la clase? (No – seguro/a de mí mismo/a)

3. ¿Está la profesora muy loca? (Sí)

4. ¿Se siente tu compañero de clase muy ansioso? (No – distraído)

5. ¿Está travieso tu hijo? (No – curioso)

6. ¿Estás muy estresado/a esta noche? (No – emocionado/a)

*With certain feelings, we use the verb "tener" (to have). Here are the conjugations of the verb "tener".

Tengo	Tenemos
Tienes	Tenéis
Tiene	Tienen

Pair the verb "tener" with the following expressions:

(mucha) hambre	To be (very) hungry
(mucha) prisa	To be in a (big) hurry
(mucha) sed	To be (very) thirsty
(mucha) suerte	To be (very) lucky
(mucha) vergüenza	To be (very) embarrassed
(mucho) calor	To be (very) hot
(mucho) cuidado	To be (very) careful
(mucho) frío	To be (very) cold
(mucho) miedo	To be (very) scared
(mucho) sueño	To be (very) sleepy
(number) años	To be (number) years old
ganas de (infinitive)	To want to do (to feel like doing) something
que (infinitive)	To have to do something
Razón	To be right

* To ask a person how old they are, say… ¿Cuántos años tiene(s)?

Práctica 14.4
Translate the following sentences to Spanish using the expressions of "tener".

1. I am cold = _____

2. She is hungry = _____

3. We are very tired. = _____

4. They have to eat. = _____

5. I have to go. = _____

6. He feels like dancing. = _____

7. She is 35 years old. = _____

8. I am (?) years old. = _____

9. Are you thirsty? = _____

10. Is she scared? = _____

Práctica 14.5
Tell how you feel in the following situations. (Note: Acabar de + infinitive means "just finished something"... por ejemplo... "Acabas de comer" means "You just finished eating")

1. Acabas de llegar a clase y hay un examen muy difíicl. ¿Cómo estás?

2. Acabas de usar una palabra incorrecta en español y todos se ríen de ti (everyone is laughing at you). ¿Cómo te sientes?

3. Estás en la playa. Hace fresco, pero no hace frío y no tienes que hacer nada. ¿Cómo te sientes?

4. Acabas de ganar la lotería. ¿Cómo te sientes?

5. Acabas de llegar a la casa después de un día largo de trabajo. ¿Cómo estás?

6. Tu amigo dice (says) que dos más dos son cinco y tú dices que dos más dos son cuatro. ¿Qué tienes?

7. Estás en el desierto y acabas de caminar por millas. ¿Cómo estás y qué tienes?

8. Estás en la oficina y hay muchos papeles en tu escritorio. El teléfono suena (is ringing) y hay un email urgente que tienes que escribir. ¿Cómo estás en este momento?

9. Son las dos de la mañana y estás en tu casa en tu cama. Hay un sonido en el patio. Ves una figura que corre por la ventana. ¿Cómo te sientes? (¿Qué tienes?)

10. Tienes una cita con la doctora a las tres y media. Ahora son las tres y cuarto. Estás en tu coche y hay mucho tráfico. ¿Cómo estás? ¿Qué tienes?

* When something hurts physically, we use the verb "doler". Since this verb means "to hurt", we don't want to say, "I hurt", "you hurt" etc. because that would mean we physically hurt someone else. So we pair the verb "doler" with an indirect object pronoun (me, te, le, nos, os, les) to show that something is painful to someone. We use only the forms "duele" or "duelen" usually to show that one or more parts hurt:

Ejemplo:

1. Me duele el ojo. = *My* eye hurts (me)... My eye is painful to me.

2. Me duelen los ojos. = *My eyes hurt (me)... My eyes are hurting me.*

3. ¿Qué le duele? = *What hurts you (formal)?*

4. ¿Qué le duelen? = *What all is hurting you (formal)?*

5. ¿Te duele la cabeza? = *Does your head hurt (informal)?*

Me duele (n)	It/they hurt(s) me
Te duele (n)	It/they hurt(s) you
Le duele (n)	It/they hurt(s) him, her
Nos duele (n)	It/they hurt(s) us
Os duele (n)	It/they hurt(s) you guys (Spain)
Les duele (n)	It/they hurt(s) you all

Names of body parts in Spanish:

El tobillo	The ankle
El brazo	The arm
La espalda	The back
El hueso	The bone
La mejilla	The cheek
El pecho	The chest
El mentón	The chin
La oreja, el oído	The (outer) ear, the (inner) ear
El codo	The elbow

El ojo	The eye
La cara	The face
El dedo	The finger
El pie	The foot
La frente	The forehead
La cabeza	The head
El corazón	The heart
La cadera	The hip
La rodilla	The knee
La pierna	The leg
El labio	The lip
La muela	The molar
La boca	The mouth
El músculo	The muscle
El cuello	The neck
La nariz	The nose
La palma (de la mano)	The palm (of the hand)
El hombro	The shoulder
La planta (del pie)	The sole (of the foot)
El estómago	The stomach
El muslo	The thigh
El pulgar	The thumb
El dedo del pie	The toe
La lengua	The tongue
El diente	The tooth
La muñeca	The wrist

Práctica 14.6
Translate the following sentences to Spanish.

1. My arm hurts = _____

2. My legs hurt = _____

3. Do your knees hurt? = _____

4. I have a headache = _____

5. Her thumb hurts. = _____

6. His toes hurt. = _____

7. What is hurting you (Ud.)? _____

8. She has a stomach ache. _____

Diálogo 14.1

Practice what you've learned by reading the dialogue aloud with your partner.

Estudiante A - ¿Por qué estás triste?

Estudiante B – No es que estoy triste. Estoy muy cansado hoy. No me siento bien.

Estudiante A - ¿Por qué estás tan cansado?

Estudiante B – Es que no me gusta cuando hace mucho calor como hace hoy. Me siento muy cansado y me duele la cabeza.

Estudiante A – Ah, sí, te comprendo. Me duele la cabeza también cuando hace mucho calor. Pero me gusta el sol. Oye, amigo, ¿tienes sed? ¿Deseas tomar un refresco en ese restaurante?

Estudiante B – No tengo sed, pero tengo hambre. Sí, te acompaño al restaurante para comer y tomar un refresco contigo. Gracias.

Estudiante A – No hay de que. Vámonos.

Diálogo 14.2

Choose one partner to be the doctor and the other to be the patient. Read your parts aloud and focus on how the patient expresses how he/she feels.

Doctor –   Buenos días, Señora, ¿Cómo está Ud. hoy? ¿Por qué está Ud. aquí para verme?

Paciente – Buenos días, Doctor. Estoy aquí porque me duele la garganta y no me siento bien.

Doctor -   ¿Tiene Ud. fiebre?

Paciente – No, doctor. No tengo fiebre.

Doctor –   Bueno. Creo que Ud. habla demasiado y es por eso que le duele la garganta. No hable más, y así Ud. va a mejorarse.

Paciente – Pero, Doctor. Soy maestra. Tengo que hablar mucho en la clase para enseñar a los estudiantes. ¿No hablar? – pues, no es posible para mí. ¿No hay otro remedio?

Doctor –   Claro que sí, Señora. Hay otro remedio. Ud. solo tiene que cambiar su profesión.

Paciente - ¿Cambiar mi profesión? Ay, ¡qué locura! Ud. es charlatán. Me voy.

Doctor –   Bueno, Señora, pero Ud. tiene que pagar antes de salir. El consejo de un doctor como yo no viene sin un precio. Adiós y que le vaya bien.

Diálogo 14.3
Choose one partner to be the son/daughter and the other to be the mother. Read your parts aloud and focus on how the son expresses how he/she feels.

Hijo(a) - Mamá, mamá.

Madre - ¿Qué te pasa, hijo(a)? ¿Qué tienes? ¿Te duele algo?

Hijo(a) - No, mamá, no me duele nada.

Madre - ¿Tienes fiebre?

Hijo(a) – No mamá, no tengo fiebre tampoco.

Madre - ¿Tienes sed? Tengo leche, jugo, agua...

Hijo(a) – No, mamá. No tengo sed. Es que..

Madre - Tienes hambre, ¿no? Bueno, hay sándwiches de jamón, fruta...

Hijo(a) – No. No tengo hambre. Es que...

Madre - ¿Tienes frío, calor, sueño...? Dime, hijo, ¿qué tienes?

Hijo(a) – Mamá, no me duele nada, no tengo fiebre, calor, frío, hambre, o sueño. Es que tengo mucha suerte y tengo ganas de decirte que eres la mejor mamá de todas.

15. Back to the Future

Using the Verb "ir" to Tell Where You Are Going and to Express a Future Action

*The verb "ir" means "to go". Here are its conjugations in the present tense.

Voy	Vamos
Vas	Vais
Va	Van

*It is usually followed by the preposition "a", meaning "to".

*If the place someone is going to is a feminine noun, we say, "a la"

    Ejemplo: Vamos a la tienda = *We are going to the store.*

    Ejemplo: Vamos a la playa = *We are going to the beach.*

*If the place someone is going to is a masculine noun, we combine "a" and "el" to "al"

    Ejemplo: Vamos al cine. = *We are going to the movies.*

    Ejemplo: Vamos al museo = *We are going to the museum.*

* We can also use the verb "ir" with an expression that means "going to do something"... and it is one way to express a future action. You conjugate the verb "ir" to match the subject, and then follow the conjugated form with "a + the infinitive". The formula looks like this:

"ir" + a + infinitive

Ejemplos:
1. Yo voy a comer = *I am going to eat.*
2. Vamos a hablar en español = *We are going to speak in Spanish.*
3. ¿Vas a ir al museo? = *Are you going to go to the museum?*

Diálogo 15.1
Read the following dialogue between two friends, Anita and Verónica. Decide which partner will read the role of Anita and who will read the part of Verónica. Read out loud to one another.

Anita: Verónica, ¿por qué sonríes?
Verónica: Sonrío porque pienso en mi viaje que voy a hacer en la semana entrante.
Anita: ¡Qué bueno! ¿Adónde vas a viajar?

Verónica: El viernes voy a viajar a San Diego. Allí voy a visitar a mi hermanita. Nosotras vamos a comer en un restaurante mexicano allí.

Anita: ¡Delicioso! ¿Y después? ¿Qué vas a hacer?

Verónica: Mi hermanita y yo vamos a tomar un crucero por México.

Anita: ¡Qué emocionante! Ahora tengo envidia. ¡Yo quiero tomar un crucero a México!

Verónica: Ja, ja. La próxima vez quizás.

Práctica 15.1:

Translate the following sentences using the formula "ir + a + infinitive"

1. They are going to swim at 2:00. =

_____

2. What are you going to do today? =

_____

3. Is he going to go to the bank? =

_____

4. Are we going to visit the museum? =

_____

5. I am going to the park. (¡Ojo!) =

_____

Práctica 15.2:

Answer the following questions using complete sentence answers.

1. ¿Adónde vas tú mañana al mediodía?

_____

2. ¿Qué vas a hacer después de clase?

_____

3. ¿Qué vas a hacer este fin de semana?

_____

4. ¿Qué vas a hacer para celebrar tu cumpleaños?

_____

Chapter 16: Naughty Verbs

Using Irregular Verbs

(Irregular "Yo" and Stem Changing "Shoe" Verbs)

*There are many irregular verbs in Spanish (meaning that the verb does not follow the pattern for conjugation that we learned in chapter 11.)

*Irregular "yo" verbs are those verbs that only have an irregular conjugation for the subject "yo". All the other conjugations work just like the regular verbs.

Ejemplo:
Conocer = to know a person, be familiar with someone or something:

Cono**zco**	Conocemos
Conoces	Conocéis
Conoce	conocen

Irregular "yo" verbs:

Verb	Translation	"yo" form (irregularity)
Hacer	To do, make	Hago
Poner	To put, to place	Pongo
Caer	To fall	Caigo
Traer	To bring	Traigo
Salir	To go out, leave	Salgo
Saber	To know (how to do something, to know a fact)	Sé
Dar	To give	Doy
Ver	To see	Veo
Conducir	To drive	Conduzco
Agradecer	To thank	Agradezco
Reconocer	To recognize	Reconozco
Ofrecer	To offer	Ofrezco
Traducir	To translate	Traduzco

Práctica 16.1:
Answer the following questions in complete sentences.

1. ¿Sabes (tú) tocar el piano?

_____

2. ¿Das (tú) el dinero al banquero?

_____

3. ¿Agradeces (tú) a tus padres?

_____

4. ¿Ves (tú) la televisión mucho?

_____

5. ¿Sales (tú) con tus amigos?

_____

Práctica 16.2
Speak with your partner. Choose to ask either the questions under column "A" or column "B".

A	**B**
1. ¿A qué hora sales de la clase?	1. ¿Qué haces los fines de semana?
2. ¿Reconoces fácilmente a las personas?	2. ¿Qué traes a una fiesta?
3. ¿Qué sabes hacer muy bien?	3. ¿Ves mucho a tus parientes (relatives)?

* Some verbs in Spanish undergo a spelling change in the stem of the verb. The stem of the verb is the middle part, or the part of the verb remaining after dropping of the ending of the verb. It may also require you to drop off the first syllable of the word if there is more than one syllable in the original infinitive.

Práctica 16.3:
Find the stem of these verbs:

1.   Dormir (to sleep) = _____

2.   Repetir (to repeat) = _____

3.   Entender (to understand) = _____

4.   Poder (to be able to, can) = _____

5.   Corregir (to correct) = _____

* There are three types of stem changes:

      1. "e" ➔ "ie" (meaning the "e" in the stem changes to "ie")

      2. "o" ➔ "ue" (meaning the "o" in the stem changes to "ue")

      3. "e" ➔ "i" (meaning the "e" in the stem changes to "i")

*These verbs are nicknamed the "shoe" or "boot" verbs because the stem change only happens with the "yo", "tú", "Ud., él, ella" , and "Uds., ellos, ellas" forms... and when you look at those forms on the chart, and draw a line around them, the figure it forms looks like a boot or shoe.

Ejemplos del grupo "e" ➔ "ie"

1. pensar

Pensar = to think	
pienso	pensamos
piensas	pensáis
piensa	piensan

2. despertar

Despertar(se) = to wake	
me despierto	nos despertamos
te despiertas	os despertáis
se despierta	se despiertan

3. divertir

Divertir(se) = to enjoy	
me divierto	nos divertimos
te diviertes	os divertís
se divierte	se divierten

4. entender

entender = to understand	
entiendo	entendemos
entiendes	entendéis
entiende	entienden

Verbs that have the "e" to "ie" stem change:

Calentar	To heat
Cerrar	To close
Comenzar	To begin
Confesar	To confess
Defender	To defend
Despertar (se)	To wake up
Divertir (se)	To enjoy oneself
Empezar	To start

Encender	To light, to ignite
Entender	To understand
Hervir	To boil
Mentir	To lie
Merendar	To have a snack
Negar	To deny
Nevar	To snow
Pensar	To think
Perder	To lose
Preferir	To prefer
Querer	To want
Sentar (se)	To sit down
Sentir (se)	To feel, to regret

Práctica 16.4:
Translate the following.

1. I am heating the water.

_____

2. We are heating the pool (la piscina).

_____

3. Do you (tú) prefer coffee or tea?

_____

4. We never lie.

_____

5. I want to go to the museum, but you guys want to go to the movie theater.

_____

6. What time does the movie begin?

_____

7. What do you all think?

_____

8. What are you (tú) thinking about?

_____

9. They always lose.

_____

10. We close the windows when it is cold.

_____

Práctica 16.5
Read the following mini story to your partner and have him/her answer the questions in parentheses as you go along. The translation and the answers to the questions are in the back of the book in the appendix section.

Juanita se despierta a las siete de la mañana. (¿Se despierta Juanita a las seis o a las siete?) **Juanita quiere ir a la playa porque hace calor.** (¿Adónde quiere ir Juanita?) **Juanita piensa mucho en las cosas que quiere llevar.** (¿Piensa Juanita en su esposo o en las cosas que quiere llevar a la playa?) **Juanita piensa en llevar una silla de playa pero prefiere llevar una toalla.** (¿Prefiere Juanita una silla de playa o una toalla?) **Juanita empieza a preparar su almuerzo.** (¿Empieza Juanita a preparar su merienda o su almuerzo?) **Juanita quiere un sándwich de jamón y fruta para su almuerzo. Pone pan, jamón y uvas en una neverita.** (¿Pone la comida en una canasta o en una neverita?) **Juanita busca las llaves de su coche, pero no las ve.** (¿Juanita ve sus llaves o no?) **Juanita se siente triste porque no va a la playa hoy sin las llaves de su coche.** (¿Se siente triste o contenta Juanita?) **Por fin, Juanita ve su mochila en el sofá. En su mochila están las llaves de su coche.** (¿Están las llaves de su coche en el sofá o en la mochila?) **Juanita se siente feliz porque hoy va a ir a la playa.** (¿Va a ir a la playa Juanita?)

Ejemplos del grupo "o" ➔ "ue"

1. almorzar   2. morir

almorzar = to have lunch		**morir = to die**	
alm**ue**rzo	almorzamos	m**ue**ro	morimos
alm**ue**rzas	almorzáis	m**ue**res	morís
alm**ue**rza	alm**ue**rzan	m**ue**re	m**ue**ren

3. * oler   4. poder

oler = to smell		Poder=to be able to	
h**ue**lo	olemos	p**ue**do	podemos
h**ue**les	oléis	p**ue**des	podéis
h**ue**le	h**ue**len	p**ue**de	p**ue**den

"o" ➔ "ue" stem changing verbs:

Acostar (se)	To go to bed
Almorzar	To have lunch
Colgar	To hang (up)
Contar	To count
Costar	To cost
Descolgar	To unhook, to unhang
Dormir	To sleep
Encontrar	To find
Llover	To rain
Morir	To die
Mostrar	To show
Mover	To move
Oler	To smell (huelo, hueles, huele, olemos, oléis, huelen)
Poder	To be able to, can
Recordar	To remember
Soñar (con)	To dream (about)
Tronar	To thunder
Volar	To fly
Volver	To return

Práctica 16.6

Translate the following to Spanish.

1. I go to bed early (temprano), but they go to bed late (tarde).

     _____

2. Do you (Ud.) smell the coffee?

     _____

3. We are returning tomorrow.

     _____

4. How much do the shirts cost?

     _____

5. I can speak in Spanish now!

     _____

6. She doesn't remember my name.

     _____

7. It's raining and thundering.

     _____

8. We sleep well when it is cold.

     _____

9. I can't find my keys (las llaves).

     _____

10. Are you moving the books to the table?

     _____

Práctica 16.7

Read the following mini story to your partner and have him/her answer the questions in parentheses as you go along. The translation to the story and answers to the questions are in the back of the book in the appendix section.

Marta siempre sueña con viajar a Puerto Vallarta. *(¿Con qué sueña Marta? ¿Viajar a Puerto Vallarta o a Acapulco?)* **A ella le encanta la playa y la cultura mexicana.** *(¿Le encanta la cultura mexicana o la cultura puertorriqueña?)* **Pero ella no puede viajar a Puerto Vallarta porque cuesta mucho dinero y ella no tiene mucho dinero.** *(¿Tiene mucho o poco dinero Marta?)* **Es que Marta ahora no tiene trabajo.** *(¿Tiene trabajo Marta?)*

Un día, Marta almuerza en una taquería y ve a su amiga, Susana. *(¿Ve Marta a su mamá o a su amiga?)* **Susana le muestra a Marta una foto de su nueva casa.** *(¿Qué hay en la foto?)* **¡Su casa nueva está en Puerto Vallarta!** *(¿Dónde está la casa nueva?)*

"Quiero encontrar a una persona para cuidar mi casa mientras no estoy allí," dice Susana. Susana necesita ayuda con su casa. *(¿Necesita Susana una persona para ayudar en la casa o para visitar la casa?)*

"Yo puedo trabajar en tu casa," le dice Marta. Marta se siente muy feliz y emocionada porque a Susana le gusta mucho la idea. *(¿Tiene Marta un trabajo ahora?)*

Ejemplos del grupo "e" ➔ "i"

1. pedir
2. reír

pedir = to ask for, order		Reír (se) =to laugh	
pido	pedimos	me río	nos reímos
pides	pedís	te ríes	os reís
pide	piden	se ríe	se ríen

3. servir　　　　　　　　　　　　　**4. medir**

Servir = to serve		Medir -= to measure	
sirvo	servimos	mido	medimos
sirves	servís	mides	medís
sirve	sirven	mide	miden

Here is a list of some "e" to "i" stem changing verbs:

Competir	To compete
Despedir (se) de	To say goodbye to
Medir	To measure
Pedir	To ask for, to order
Reír (se) (de)	To laugh (at)
Repetir	To repeat
Seguir	To follow
Servir	To serve
Sonreír (se)	To smile
Vestir (se)	To get dressed

Práctica 16. 8

Translate the sentences to Spanish.

1. I say goodbye to my friends.

_____

2. Does the waiter (el mozo) serve the food?

_____

3. My friends laugh at the joke (el chiste).

_____

4. Are you following the rules (las reglas)?

_____

5. Who is next (Who follows)?

_____

6. We are ordering pizza and sodas.

_____

7. I get dressed at 6am.

_____

8. The students repeat the words with the teacher.

_____

9. We smile when we see our friends..

_____

10. I compete in many sports.

_____

Práctica 16.9

Choose one partner to read the even numbered sentences and the other partner to read the odd numbered sentences. As you read the sentence to your partner, choose the information in parenthesis that you think makes the entire sentence true about your partner.   Afterwards, have your partner tell you if what you chose was "cierto" or "falso" about him/her.

1. Compites en (muchos / pocos) deportes.

2. Generalmente sirves comidas con   (mucha carne / muchos vegetales).

3. (Nunca / Siempre / De vez en cuando) pides un vaso de vino con tu comida.

4. Generalmente tomas (mucho / poco) tiempo para vestirte por las mañanas.

5. Sonríes (mucho / poco).

6. Cuando termina una fiesta, generalmente (te despides / no te despides) de tus

   amigos.

7. Mides (dos veces / solo una vez) antes de hacer algo o construir algo.

8. (Siempre, A veces, Nunca) sigues las reglas.

9. Duermes (menos de / más de) ocho horas cada noche.

10. (Puedes / No puedes) tocar un instrumento.

11. (Siempre / De vez en cuando / Nunca) cuelgas la ropa en el armario.

12. Te acuestas (tarde / temprano).

13. Te despiertas (tarde / temprano).

14. (Recuerdas / No recuerdas) mucho de tu niñez (childhood).

15. Generalmente almuerzas (en casa / en un restaurante).

16. (Cierras / Abres) las ventanas cuando estás en la casa durante el día.

17. Te diviertes (mucho / poco) en las fiestas donde hay mucha gente.

18. (Te gusta / No te gusta) cuando nieva.

19. (Te gusta / No te gusta) cuando llueve.

20. Prefieres el color (rojo / verde / amarillo / negro / anaranjado / blanco / azul).

Chapter 17: Simon Says...

Giving Commands and Making Polite Requests

*To tell someone what to do (or what not to do), we have to make a slight change to the present tense conjugation of a verb.

*We can give a command to (tú, Ud., Uds. and nosotros). In this chapter, we only focus on how to give a command to "Ud." and "Uds." because they are the commands we use most often.

*These are the steps you take to form a command:
1. Find the "yo" form of the verb in the present tense.
2. Drop the final ending "o" off of the conjugation and add the following endings based on the person TO WHOM you are speaking:
   * For –AR verbs, add "-e" when talking to Ud. and "-en" when talking to Uds.
   * For –ER and –IR verbs, add "a" when talking to Ud. and "-an" when talking to Uds.
   * To tell someone NOT TO DO something, just add "No" before the command form of the verb.

Ejemplos:

1. Hable Ud. en español. = *Speak in Spanish (talking to Ud.)*
2. No hable Ud. en inglés. = *Don't speak in English (talking to Ud.)*
3. Escuchen Uds. a la profesora. = *Listen to the teacher. (talking to Uds.)*
4. No duerman en la clase. = *Don't sleep in the class. (talking to Uds.)*
5. Hagan muchas preguntas. = *Ask many questions. (talking to Uds.)*

Práctica 17.1
Change the infinitive to a command according to the subject given. Break the process down into step one and step two as mentioned in the description above.

(NOTE: With the verbs that have a reflexive pronoun, the pronoun is attached onto the end of the command if it's affirmative (if you're telling someone what TO DO). If you're telling someone what NOT TO DO, you place the reflexive pronoun before the command).

Ejemplo: Lávese las manos. = Wash your hands.
No se lave las manos. = Don't wash your hands.

Infinitive	"Yo" form of verb	Ud. command form	Uds. command Form
1. comer (eat)	*Como*	*Coma*	*Coman*

2. escuchar (listen)			
3. sentar(se) (sit)			
4. abrir (open)			
5. decir (say, tell)			
6. leer (read)			
7. correr (run)			
8. beber (drink)			
9. parar (stop)			
10. doblar (turn)			
11. tomar (take)			
12. mirar (watch)			
13. llamar (call)			
14. quitar(se) (take off)			
15. lavar(se) (wash)			

* There are 5 irregular verbs that don't follow this pattern:

Infinitive	English	Ud. command form	Uds. command Form
1. ir	Go	vaya	Vayan
2. ser	Be	Sea	Sean
3. Estar	Be	Esté	Estén
4. Dar	Give	Dé	Den
5. Saber	Know	Sepa	Sepan

*Verbs that end in –CAR, -GAR, or –ZAR have a slight spell change so the written form matches how the word should be pronounced.

*Verbs ending in –CAR will have the ending –que for Ud. and –quen for Uds.
*Verbs ending in –GAR will have the ending –gue for Ud. and –guen for Uds.
*Verbs ending in –ZAR will have the ending –ce for Ud. and –cen for Uds.

Práctica 17. 2
Change the infinitive to a command according to the subject given. Break the process down into step one and step two as mentioned in the description above.

Infinitive	"Yo" form of verb	Ud. command form	Uds. command Form
1. llegar (arrive)	Llego	Llegue	lleguen
2. buscar (look for)			
3. almorzar (have lunch)			
4. pagar (pay)			
5. tocar (play, an instrument)			
6. comenzar (begin)			

Práctica 17.3
Translate the following to Spanish. Give the following commands to Ud.

1. Don't run! _____

2. Pay the bill (la cuenta). _____

3. Don't sell the house. _____

4. Turn to the right (la derecha). _____

5. Sit down and open the book. _____

6. Don't sleep now. _____

Práctica 17.4
Translate the following to Spanish. Give the following commands to Uds.

1. Go to the museum. _____

2. Don't give the money to the server. _____

3. Watch the movie. _____

4. Turn to the left (la izquierda). _____

5. Don't be sad. _____

6. Go to bed early. _____

Práctica 17.5
Choose one partner to read the even numbered sentences and the other partner to read the odd numbered sentences. The person reading the sentence is playing the role of the patient and the other person is the doctor. After the "patient" reads the symptoms or problems he/she is having, the doctor needs to respond with a command (it doesn't have to be just one!) that will help the patient solve his/her problem(s). Remember that you can tell the patient what to do as well as what NOT to do!

1. Doctor(a), siempre estoy muy cansado(a). No tengo mucha energía durante el día. Duermo cuatro a seis horas cada noche. A veces hago ejercicio.

2. Doctor(a), me duele mucho el estómago. Como tres comidas cada día y tomo mucha leche. Me gusta mucho el queso y me encantan los huevos, y por eso como mucho queso y huevos.

3. Doctor(a), me siento muy ansioso(a) todo el tiempo. No me puedo concentrar porque estoy muy nervioso(a). Por lo menos (at least), yo puedo hacer mi trabajo, y trabajo seis días cada semana y cada día trabajo nueve o diez horas. No veo mucho a mis amigos o a mi familia, pero me gusta mucho mi trabajo y estoy contento(a) en la oficina donde trabajo.

4. Doctor(a), me siento horrible. Mis ojos me duelen, la cabeza me duele y estornudo (I sneeze) todo el día. Me duele la garganta y tengo mucho sueño.

Práctica 17. 6
Play a game of Simon Says with your partner. Start with "Simón Dice...". Here is a list of commands you can have your partner do.

1. Toque el brazo, la cabeza, el ojo, la rodilla etc. (touch your arm, head, eye, kneee, etc.)
2. Diga su nombre. (Say your name).
3. Escriba su nombre. (Write your name).
4. Dibuje un círculo, un cuadrado, un triángulo, un diamante etc. (Draw a circle, square, triangle, diamond, etc.)
5. Baile. (Dance).
6. Cante una canción. (Sing a song).
7. Salte. (Jump).
8. Quítese el zapato. (Take off your shoe).
9. Póngase el zapato. (Put on the shoe.)
10. Siéntese. (Sit down).

11. Levántese. (Stand up / Get up).
12. Cierre los ojos. (Close your eyes).
13. Abra los ojos. (Open your eyes).
14. Silbe. (Whistle).
15. Salude a un(a) compañero(a) de clase. (Greet/Wave to a classmate).

Chapter 18: Time Traveling to the Past

Expressing Actions in the Past – Using the Imperfect Tense

* There are TWO past tenses in Spanish:
      a. The Imperfect ~ Expresses ongoing or continuous action in the past
      b. The Preterite ~ Expresses a completed action in the past

Compare and Contrast the Imperfect and Preterite Tenses:

THE USES OF THE IMPERFECT	THE USES OF THE PRETERITE
1. Continuous action in the past: Example: I *used to live* in Burbank. Ejemplo: Yo *vivía* en Burbank.	**1. Complete, one-time action in the past:** Example: I *opened* the door. Ejemplo: Yo *abrí* la puerta.
2. Repeated action in the past: Example: We *went* to the beach every summer. Ejemplo: *Íbamos* a la playa cada verano.	**2. Fixed number of actions in the past.** Example: She *read* that book twice. Ejemplo: Ella *leyó* ese libro dos veces.
3. Time in the past. Example: It *was* five thirty. Ejemplo: *Eran* las cinco y media.	**3. Action that took place in an enclosed amount of time:** Example: I *lived* there for two years. Ejemplo: Yo *viví* allí por dos años.
4. Description of a person or thing in the past. Example: I *was* small for my age. Ejemplo: Yo *era* pequeña para mi edad. Example: She *was* a very nice person. Ejemplo: Ella *era* una persona muy simpática.	
5. Description of the circumstances surrounding another event. Example: They *were talking* when he arrived. Ejemplo: Ellos *hablaban* cuando él llegó.	
6. Description of a mental or emotional action. Example: I *liked* skating. Ejemplo: Me *gustaba* patinar. Example: I *knew* him very well. Ejemplo: Lo *conocía* muy bien.	

Práctica 18.1
Decide if the italicized verb would be in the imperfect or the preterite.

1. I *wanted* to be an actress.	Imperfect	Preterite
2. She *went* to Paris last summer.	Imperfect	Preterite
3. They *used to sing* in a choir.	Imperfect	Preterite
4. The wind *was blowing* when the fire started.	Imperfect	Preterite
5. She *closed* the door when she left.	Imperfect	Preterite
6. I always *ate* cereal for breakfast.	Imperfect	Preterite

*Just like we did with the present tense, we need to change the endings of the verb to match the subjects. The imperfect tense has its own set of endings.

Imperfect Tense Endings:

-AR

Singular	Plural
- aba	**-ábamos**
-abas	**-abais**
-aba	**-aban**

Práctica 18.2
Fill in the blank with the imperfect tense of the –AR verb that matches the subject.

1. Ella (mirar) _____ = *She used to watch.*

2. Yo (hablar) _____ = *I was speaking/talking.*

3. Ellos (trabajar) = _____ = *They used to work.*

4. Nosotros (cantar) = _____ = *We used to sing.*

5. ¿(Escuchar) _____ tú? = *Were you listening?*

6. Yo (viajar) _____ cada verano. = *I traveled every summer.*

7. Vosotros (trabajar) _____ allí. = *You guys used to work there.*

8. Tú (almorzar) _____ a las dos cada día. = *You ate lunch at 2:00 every day.*

9. A María le (gustar) _____ leer. = *María liked to read.*

10. Yo (pensar) _____ en el futuro. = *I thought about the future.*

-ER, -IR

Singular	Plural
- ía	- íamos
- ías	- íais
- ía	- ían

Práctica 18.3
Fill in the blank with the imperfect tense of the –AR verb that matches the subject.

1. Ella (vivir) en Perú. _____ = *She used to live in Peru.*

2. Yo (escribir) _____ = *I was writing.*

3. Ellos (comprender) = _____ = *They understood.*

4. Nosotros (recibir) = _____ = *We used to receive.*

5. ¿Lo (saber) _____ tú? = *Did you know it?*

6. Mis padres (leer) _____ cada noche. = *My parents used to read each night.*

7. Vosotros (creer) _____ el cuento. = *You guys believed the story.*

8. Tú (repetir) _____ las palabras. = *You were repeating the words.*

9. Carlos (vender) _____ casas. = *Carlos used to sell houses.*

10. Tú y yo (abrir) _____ las ventanas. = *You and I were opening the windows.*

*There are only three naughty (or irregular) verbs in the imperfect tense! They are "ser", "ir", and "ver".

1. SER = to be

era	éramos
eras	erais
era	eran

2. IR = To go

iba	íbamos
ibas	ibais
iba	iban

3. Ver = To see

veía	veíamos
veías	veíais
veía	veían

Práctica 18.4
Translate the following to Spanish

1. I used to be tall. = _____

2. She used to go to the beach on weekends. = _____

   _____

3. They used to see the dog. = _____

4. It was 1:00. = _____

5. It was 6:30. = _____

6. We used to go to the park. = _____

7. Were you short? _____

8. I always used to see the green house. _____

   _____

9. My mom used to be very active in the school. _____

   _____

10. Did all of you used to go to the movie theater every weekend? _____

    _____

Práctica 18.5

Practice using the imperfect tense by answering the following questions. Use this bank of vocabulary to help you:

La leche = the milk	Obedecer = to obey	Las películas = The films/movies	El cine = The movie theater	Grande = Big
Pequeño = Small	La edad = The age	Colorear = To color	Los crayones = The crayons	Visitar = To viist
El parque = The park	Saber = To know (how to do something)	montar en bicicleta= To ride a bike	De vez en cuando= Once in a while	Jugar = to play
Viajar = To travel	Mudarse = To move (from one home to another)	Tímido = shy	Acampar= To camp	La tienda de acampar= The tent
Los abuelos= The grandparents	Tener miedo = To be afraid	Los monstruos= The monsters	Querer= To want	El astronauto= The astronaut

Instructions: For each of the following questions, start with the phrase, "Cuando tenías 10 años..." which means, "When you were 10 years old..."

Pregunta	Yo	Mi compañero(a)
(Ejemplo) 1. ¿Vivías en California?	sí	
2. ¿Bebías leche?		
3. ¿Escuchabas música clásica?		
4. ¿Te gustaba leer?		
5. ¿Obedecías a tus padres?		
6. ¿Veías muchas películas en el cine?		
7. ¿Eras grande o pequeño(a) para tu edad?		
8. ¿Te gustaba colorear con crayones?		
9. ¿Visitabas mucho el parque?		
10. ¿Sabías montar en bicicleta?		
11. ¿Ibas a los museos de vez en cuando?		
12. ¿Jugabas con amigos?		
13. ¿Tocabas un instrumento?		

14. ¿Viajabas mucho?		
15. ¿Te mudabas mucho?		
16. ¿Eras tímido(a)?		
17. ¿Acampabas en una tienda de acampar?		
18. ¿Visitabas a tus abuelos?		
19. ¿Tenías miedo de los monstruos?		
20. ¿Querías ser astronauta?		

Diálogo 18.1

Decide who will play the role of Elisa and who will play Mateo as they are out on a date. Read your roles out loud. Focus on how the imperfect tense is used to express what the person used to be like in the past.

Elisa – Mateo, quiero saber cómo eras cuando eras joven. ¿Eras tan amable cuando eras joven?

Mateo – Pues, no sé nada de esto, pero sí, más o menos... era amable con todos. No era tímido.

Elisa - Siempre eras muy lindo, ¿no? Porque eres muy guapo ahora.

Mateo- Gracias, Elisa. Creo que sí. Siempre era muy lindo. Es lo que dice mi mamá.

Elisa - Y, ¿qué te gustaba hacer? ¿Jugabas mucho con tus amigos?

Mateo- Bueno, sí. Siempre jugaba con la misma chica. Se llamaba Susana. Era una chica muy linda y muy simpática.

Elisa - ¿Una chica? ¿Susana?

Mateo - Sí. Susana era una chica fabulosa. Era muy inteligente y siempre ganaba en los juegos. Ella cenaba con mi familia casi todos los días.

Elisa - ¿Una chica fabulosa, eh? ¿Siempre iba a tu casa y pasaba tiempo con tu familia?

Mateo - Ah, sí. Tenía el pelo largo y los ojos grandes y...

Elisa - Bueno, Mateo. Creo que ahora yo sé bastante información de cuando eras joven. Es mejor hablar del futuro. ¿No crees?

Chapter 19: You Were There

Expressing Completed Actions in the Past –

Using the Preterite Tense

Some key words that often accompany the preterite tense:

Anoche	Last night
Anteayer	The day before yesterday
Ayer	Yesterday
El/la (año, mes, semana etc.) pasado(a)	Last (year, month, week etc.)
Hace +(period of time) Ejemplo: Hace un año	(a period of time) ago Example: A year ago

*The preterite tense is formed by dropping of the ending of the infinitive and adding the following:

-AR Verb Endings in the Preterite Tense

Singular		Plural	
(yo)	- é	(nosotros)	- amos
(tú)	- aste	(vosotros)	- asteis
(Ud., él, ella)	- ó	(Uds., ellos, ellas)	- aron

Práctica 19.1
Fill in the blank with the appropriate preterite tense form of the verb according to the subject.

1. Yo (hablar) con la profesora. _hablé_____. = *I spoke with the teacher.*

2. Ella (cantar) en la clase. ___cantó_____. = *She sang in the class.*

3. Nosotros (trabajar) ____trabajamos_____ ayer. = *We worked yesterday.*

4. Ellos (bailar) _____bailaron_____ en la fiesta. = *They danced at the party.*

5. Tú (viajar) _viajaste_ el verano pasado. = *You traveled last summer.*

-ER AND -IR Verb Endings in the Preterite Tense

Singular		Plural	
(yo)	**- í**	(nosotros)	**- imos**
(tú)	**- iste**	(vosotros)	**- isteis**
(Ud., él, ella)	**- ió**	(Uds., ellos, ellas)	**- ieron**

Práctica 19.2
Fill in the blank with the appropriate preterite tense form of the verb according to the subject.

1. Yo (correr) _corrí_ ayer. = *I ran yesterday.*
2. Ella (vivir) _vivió_ en Argentina. = *She lived in Argentina.*
3. Nosotros (comer) _comimos_ allí. = *We ate there.*
4. Ellos (abrir) _abrieron_ la ventana. = *They opened the window.*
5. Tú (vender) _vendiste_ tu casa. = *You sold your house.*

*The preterite tense has many naughty (irregular) verbs that you just need to memorize. The following are the conjugations of various high-frequency verbs and the groups in which they belong:

Spell-Changing Verbs (Verbs ending in –car, -gar, -zar)

* These verbs have a spell change just like the commands did. They end in –CAR, -GAR, -ZAR and require a spell change in the "Yo" form only in order for the word to be written as it is pronounced.

English Infini- tive	Spanish Infinitive	Yo	Tú	Ud., él, ella	Nosotros	Vosotros	Ellos, Ellas, Uds.
To arrive	Llegar	*Llegué*	Llegaste	Llegó	Llegamos	Llegasteis	llegaron
To be mistaken	Equivocar(se)	*Me equivoqué*	Te equivocaste	Se equivocó	Nos equivocamos	Os equivocasteis	Se equivocaron
To begin	Comenzar	*Comencé*	Comenzaste	Comenzó	Comenzamos	Comenzasteis	Comenzaron
To cross	cruzar	*Crucé*	Cruzaste	Cruzó	Cruzamos	Cruzasteis	Cruzaron

To deliver, hand over	Entregar	*Entregué*	Entregaste	Entregó	Entregamos	Entregasteis	Entregaron
To enjoy	Gozar	*Gocé*	Gozaste	Gozó	Gozamos	Gozasteis	Gozaron
To explain	Explicar	*Expliqué*	Explicaste	Explicó	Explicamos	Explicasteis	Explicaron
To hug	Abrazar	*Abracé*	Abrazaste	Abrazó	Abrazamos	Abrazasteis	Abrazaron
To load	Cargar	*Cargué*	Cargaste	Cargó	Cargamos	Cargasteis	Cargaron
To look for	Buscar	*Busqué*	Buscaste	Buscó	Buscamos	Buscasteis	Buscaron
To pay	Pagar	*Pagué*	Pagaste	Pagó	Pagamos	Pagasteis	Pagaron
To play (a game, sport)	Jugar	*Jugué*	jugaste	Jugó	Jugamos	Jugasteis	Jugaron
To play (an instrument)	Tocar	*Toqué*	Tocaste	Tocó	Tocamos	Tocasteis	Tocaron
To take out	Sacar	*Saqué*	Sacaste	Sacó	Sacamos	Sacasteis	Sacaron

Práctica 19.3

Choose to read either the odd or even numbers. Read the questions with your partner, and have your partner respond using comlete sentence answers and the information provided.

Ejemplo:

¿Llegaste temprano o tarde a clase? (temprano)
Llegué temprano a clase.

1. ¿Quién sacó la basura (the trash)? (Yo)

   _____

2. ¿Qué jugaste ayer? (al tenis)

   _____

3. ¿Por cuánto tiempo tocaste el piano? (tres años)

   _____

4. ¿ Cuánto pagaste por la comida? (30 dólares)

   _____

5. ¿Quiénes llegaron? (Miguel y Sara)

   _____

6. ¿Qué entregaste? (mi pasaporte)

   _____

Verbs that change the "I" to "y"

*These verbs change what would normally be an "I" to a "y" in the conjugations for the "Ud., él, ella" and "Uds, ellos, ellas) forms of the verbs. This change occurs to avoid having a tripthing (three vowels placed right next to each other).

English Infinitive	Spanish Infinitive	Yo	Tú	Ud., él, ella	Nosotros	Vosotros	Ellos, Ellas, Uds.
To believe	Creer	Creí	Creíste	*Creyó*	Creímos	Creísteis	*Creyeron*
To fall	Caer	Caí	Caíste	*Cayó*	Caímos	Caísteis	*Cayeron*
To hear	Oír	Oí	Oíste	*Oyó*	Oímos	Oísteis	*Oyeron*
To read	Leer	Leí	Leíste	*Leyó*	Leímos	Leísteis	*Leyeron*

Práctica 19.4

Choose to read either the odd or even numbers. Read the questions with your partner, and have your partner respond using complete sentence answers and the information provided.

1. ¿Jugaste al fútbol ayer? (no, al béisbol)

_____

2. ¿Oíste las noticias de hoy? (Sí)

_____

3. ¿A quién abrazaste esta mañana? (a mi esposo/a).

_____

4. ¿Qué leíste recientemente? (un libro de aventuras)

_____

5. ¿Gozaste esta clase? (Claro que sí) ☺

_____

6. ¿A qué hora comenzó la clase esta noche? (a las 7:00)

_____

7. ¿Qué buscaste en ese diccionario? (una palabra nueva)

_____

8. ¿Quién se equivocó con la información? (Yo)

_____

Stem Changing Verbs

*Just like in the present tense, the preterite tense has stem changing verbs. But these verbs do not form a shoe pattern. The change takes place only in the third person singular and plural forms (the Ud., él, ella, and Uds., ellos, ellas forms).

*These verbs were stem changing verbs from the present tense that ended with "-ir".

*There are two stem changes that take place – either from "e" to "i" or "o" to "u".

English Infinitive	Spanish Infinitive	Yo	Tú	Ud., él, ella	Nosotros	Vosotros	Ellos, Ellas, Uds.
To ask for, order	Pedir	Pedí	Pediste	Pidió	Pedimos	Pedisteis	Pidieron
To enjoy oneself	Divertir(se)	Me divertí	Te divertiste	Se divirtió	Nos divertimos	Os divertisteis	Se divirtieron
To feel	Sentir(se)	Me sentí	Te sentiste	Se sintió	Nos sentimos	Os sentisteis	Se sintieron
To laugh	Reír	Reí	Reíste	Rió	Reímos	Reísteis	Rieron
To lie	Mentir	Mentí	Mentiste	Mintió	Mentimos	Mentisteis	Mintieron
To prefer	Preferir	Preferí	Preferiste	Prefirió	Preferimos	Preferisteis	Prefirieron
To repeat	Repetir	Repetí	Repetiste	Repitió	Repetimos	Repetisteis	Repitieron
To serve	Servir	Serví	Serviste	Sirvió	Servimos	Servisteis	Sirvieron
To sleep	Dormir	Dormí	Dormiste	Durmió	Dormimos	Dormisteis	Durmieron
To smile	Sonreír	Sonreí	Sonreíste	Sonrió	Sonreímos	Sonreísteis	Sonrieron

Práctica 19.5
Choose to read either the odd or even numbers. Read the questions with your partner, and have your partner respond using comlete sentence answers and the information provided.

1. ¿De qué se rió tu hermano? (del chiste)

_____

2. ¿Quiénes repitieron las palabras nuevas? (los estudiantes)

_____

3. ¿Cómo te sentiste en la clase anoche? (muy nervioso/a)

_____

4. ¿Cómo durmieron Uds. anoche? (bien)

_____

5. ¿Quién sirvió la comida? (el mesero)

_____

6. ¿Te divertiste en la fiesta? (Sí)

_____

7. ¿Qué pidieron Uds.? (yo, un taco; mi esposo, una torta)

_____

8. ¿Cuál prefirieron Uds.? (yo, el libro; mi amiga, la película)

_____

Completely irregular verbs

*The preterite tense also has many completely irregular verbs. The bad news is that you just have to memorize these forms in order to use them. The good news is that the more you use them and practice them, the easier they are!

*One thing that might make this process of memorization easier is to note that the "yo" form sets the pattern. All the other forms are similar to the "yo" form. So, start with memorizing just the "yo" form and work your way along.

*Another good way to practice the preterite tense is to keep a daily journal. Write in Spanish (using the preterite tense, of course) at least three things you did during the day. Or, make a list as you go through your day if that suits you better! However you do it, journaling is a great way to use your language when you can't talk with your partner (or a heritage speaker) for practice. ☺

English Infinitive	Spanish Infinitive	Yo	Tú	Ud., él, ella	Nosotros	Vosotros	Ellos, Ellas, Uds.
To be	Ser	Fui	Fuiste	Fue	Fuimos	Fuisteis	Fueron
To be	Estar	Estuve	Estuviste	Estuvo	Estuvimos	Estuvisteis	Estuvieron
To be able to, can	Poder	Pude	Pudiste	Pudo	Pudimos	Pudisteis	Pudieron
to bring	Traer	Traje	Trajiste	Trajo	Trajimos	Trajisteis	Trajeron
To come	Venir	Vine	Viniste	Vino	Vinimos	Vinisteis	Vinieron
To do, make	Hacer	Hice	Hiciste	Hizo	Hicimos	Hicisteis	Hicieron
To drive	Conducir	Conduje	Condujiste	Condujo	Condujimos	Condujisteis	Condujeron
To give	Dar	Di	Diste	Dio	Dimos	Disteis	Dieron
To go	Ir	Fui	Fuiste	Fue	Fuimos	Fuisteis	Fueron
To have	Tener	Tuve	Tuviste	Tuvo	Tuvimos	Tuvisteis	Tuvieron
To know (To find out)	Saber	Supe	Supiste	Supo	Supimos	Supisteis	Supieron
To put, place	Poner	Puse	Pusiste	Puso	Pusimos	Pusisteis	Pusieron

To say, tell	Decir	Dije	Dijiste	Dijo	Dijimos	Dijisteis	Dijeron
To translate	Traducir	Traduje	Tradujiste	Tradujo	Tradujimos	Tradujisteis	Tradujeron
To want, wish, desire	Querer	Quise	Quisiste	Quiso	Quisimos	Quisisteis	Quisieron

Práctica 19.6

Choose to read either the odd or even numbers. Read the questions with your partner, and have your partner respond using comlete sentence answers and the information provided.

1. ¿Condujiste tu coche para ir a clase esta noche? (Sí)

_____

2. ¿Quién trajo su libro a clase? (Todos)

_____

3. ¿Tuviste que trabajar hoy? (Sí)

_____

4. ¿Qué película viste anoche? (una película romántica)

_____

5. ¿Dónde estuvieron Uds. anoche? (en casa)

_____

6. ¿Adónde fueron Uds. ayer por la tarde? (al parque)

_____

7. ¿Pudiste comprender la pregunta? (No)

_____

8. ¿De quién supiste el secreto? (de Juana)

_____

9. ¿Qué dijo el señor? (que la tienda está allí)

_____

10. ¿Dónde pusiste los documentos? (en la mesa)

_____

Práctica 19.7

Read the following story and see if you can understand by answering the questions that follow. The translation of the story and the answers to the questions are located in the appendix. Note that some words are defined below the story; those defined have a footnote.

El caracol [1]mágico

    Cada verano mis padres, mi hermano y yo visitábamos a nuestros abuelos que vivían en una casa muy pequeña cerca de la playa. Durante los días, mi hermano y yo siempre nadábamos en el océano mientras [2]los adultos descansaban en la casa jugando ajedrez [3] o leyendo novelas[4]. Pero, por las noches, mi abuela siempre nos contaba [5]historias del pasado. Una noche, nos dijo un secreto que todavía me fascina[6].

    Una noche durante un verano muy largo, cuando ella tenía dieciséis años, ella decidió dar una vuelta por la orilla del océano[7]. Eran las siete de la noche y era una noche tranquila, unos minutos después de la puesta del sol[8]. Mientras mi abuela caminaba por la arena, de repente ella oyó una voz bonita cantando lentamente una canción muy interesante. Pero, mi abuela no vio a nadie en la playa. Solo estaba ella[9] y un caracol en la arena[10]. Pero ese caracol era muy raro, de un color muy bonito...un azul claro con rayas verdes y rojas y con un círculo amarillo. Mi abuela lo miró con más cuidado y vio que en ese círculo amarillo, el caracol tenía unos ojos muy negros y una boca pequeña. En este momento, el caracol le dijo a mi abuela, "Qué cosa quieres más de todo el mundo? Yo puedo darte una cosa, pero solamente una...solo tienes que decirme y yo voy a dártelo [11]ahora mismo... aquí en esta playa y en este momento. Tienes que decidir rápidamente porque no puedo quedarme aquí por mucho tiempo[12]. Yo soy un caracol mágico y así que tú me encontraste[13], tú puedes recibir tu deseo más importante del mundo. Dime, chica...¿qué quieres? Cuéntame de lo que hay en tu corazón[14]." Pues, mi abuela no se asustó[15]. Ella le pidió al caracol mágico una casa pequeña cerca de la playa con el hombre de sus sueños adentro. Y ¿sabes qué? El caracol le dio su deseo, y así es que mi abuela conoció a mi abuelo, el hombre de sus sueños viviendo en la casa pequeña cerca de la playa.

---

[1] The shell

[2] while

[3] playing chess

[4] reading novels

[5] told us

[6] still fascinates me

[7] to take a walk along the shore of the ocean

[8] some minutes after sunset

[9] There was only herself

[10] the sand

[11] I'm going to give it to you

[12] I can't stay here for long

[13] Since you found me

[14] Tell me what is in your heart

[15] didn't get scared

Práctica 19.7
Say whether the statements below are true or false about the story you just read.

1. La abuela del narrador vive en la ciudad.
2. Cada noche la abuela le contaba historias a la familia.
3. La historia que cuenta la abuela esa noche es la historia cómo la abuela conoció al abuelo.
4. La abuela encontró el caracol en una casa pequeña cerca del océano.
5. El caracol pudo darle a la abuela tres deseos.
6. La abuela tuvo miedo del caracol.
7. La abuela recibió su deseo.

Práctica 19.8
Read the following story and see if you can understand by answering the questions that follow. The translation of the story and the answers to the questions are located in the appendix.

Una visita con una amiga

Me llamo Carolina. Vivo en un apartamento en Miami y soy secretaria. Trabajo con un abogado muy trabajador y casi nunca tengo tiempo libre. Pero, ayer, por fin, tuve tiempo para visitar a una vieja amiga mía. Ella vive en un apartamento en la ciudad. Hacía muchos años que no la veía. Mi amiga se llama Teresa y nos conocimos hace diez años en la universidad.

Llegué a su apartamento a las diez de la mañana. Ella era tan bonita como la recordaba. Tenía el pelo largo y rubio y los ojos grandes y cafés. Su apartamento era pequeño pero bonito. A ella le gusta la naturaleza y por eso había muchas plantas y flores en su apartamento.

Hablamos en su apartamento por un rato, y después decidimos ir a comer en un restaurante para el almuerzo. Fuimos a un restaurante japonés porque a nosotras dos nos gusta mucho el sushi. Nos sentamos en una mesa redonda y miramos el menú. Fue entonces cuando entró un hombre alto. Llevaba un traje y una corbata morada oscura. (El morado oscuro es el color favorito de mi amiga.) Mi amiga lo miraba mientras el hombre se sentó en una silla en la mesa con nosotras. ¡Qué sorpresa! Mi amiga no me dijo nada pero empezó a hablar con él. Le dijo su nombre y el hombre le dijo el suyo. Pasaron unos minutos y yo me sentaba allí en silencio mirando esta escena muy interesante.

Después de un rato, el mesero llegó con las bebidas. ¿Crees tú que terminó así su conversación? Yo, sí... lo creí en ese momento. ¡Pero no fue así! Mi amiga pidió nuestro almuerzo sin consultarme. No me habló y no me miró. El mesero salió, y los dos continuaron hablando. Me dio tanta sorpresa que no les dije nada. Me sentaba en silencio. Los dos continuaron conversando con mucha energía y entusiasmo. Hablaron de los deportes, sus viajes, sus trabajos, y mientras tanto yo no hablé. Comimos juntos mientras ellos dos hablaron más de sus intereses y sus familias y sus deseos para el futuro. Por fin, el camarero nos trajo la cuenta. El hombre le dio las gracias por todo, y salió. Mi amiga por fin me miró y se sonrió.

- "¿Qué crees tú?" Me dijo ella.

- "Qué debo pensar?" Le pregunté, incrédula.

Entonces me explicó todo. Ella había arreglado una cita con ese hombre por internet. Tenía miedo de conocerle en persona sin otra persona allí para protegerla. Decidió tener una cita con él y una visita conmigo a la vez.

"¿Qué piensas de él?" Me preguntó ella. "No sé nada de él, " le dije, "Pero de ti, tengo una opinión completamente diferente." Me levanté de la silla, dejé dinero en la mesa, y salí.

Práctica 19.8
Choose the best answer based upon the story you just read.

1. ¿Cómo se llama la amiga?
    A. Susana
    B. Teresa
    C. Carolina
    D. No menciona el nombre

2. ¿Dónde vive la amiga?
    A. en Los Ángeles
    B. en una ciudad en Miami
    C. en México
    D. en Tejas

3. ¿Adónde fueron las dos chicas para almorzar?

    A. en el apartamento de Teresa
    B. en un restaurante chino
    C. en la cafetería donde trabaja Carolina
    D. en un restaurante japonés

4. ¿Quién llegó en el restaurante?
    A. Otra amiga de las chicas
    B. Un hombre bajo
    C. Un hombre alto
    D. Una mujer bonita

5. ¿Por qué estuvo allí el hombre y por qué se sentó en la misma mesa?
    A. Estuvo allí porque tenía una cita con Teresa
    B. Estuvo allí porque era amigo de Teresa
    C. Estuvo allí porque era amigo de Teresa y Carolina de la universidad.
    D. No menciona por qué estuvo allí.

6. ¿Qué hizo la narradora al fin de la historia?

    A. Hizo una cita con el hombre alto.
    B. Recibió un trabajo del hombre y salió con él.
    C. Continuó su conversación y visita con su amiga.
    D. Se enojó y salió del restaurante.

Chapter 20: Will It Cost an Arm and a Leg Or

An Eye From Your Face?

Idiomatic Expressions and Other Useful Phrases

*Idiomatic expressions are phrases that do not translate directly from one language to the other. If we say in English, "It"s raining cats and dogs", we understand that it must be raining very heavily. If you translate that phrase directly to Spanish and say something like, "Llueve gatos y perros", you'll get very puzzled expressions and lots of giggles. The English expression, "It will cost an arm and a leg" is a little different in Spanish, though not by too much. In Spanish, the equivalent translates as "It'll cost you an eye from your face." Below is a list of some of these phrases – our English phrase and the equivalent Spanish meaning (not the direct translation).

Idiomatic Expressions

English Phrase	Spanish Equivalent
A clean slate	Borrón y cuenta nueva
A friend in need is a friend indeed	Amigo en la adversidad, es amigo de verdad
A good deed is never lost	Haz bien y no mires a quién
A lot	Un montón
A picture is worth a thousand words	Vale más una imagen que mil palabras
A place for everything and everything in its place	Un lugar para cada cosa y cada cosa en su lugar
All that glitters is not gold	No todo lo que brilla es oro.
An apple a day keeps the doctor away	La mejor medicina es la buena comida
Ask and you shall receive	Quien tiene lengua, a Roma llega
At the end of the day (When all is said and done)	A fin de cuentas (or) al fin y al cabo
Behind someone's back	A las espaldas de alguien
Better late than never	Más vale tarde que nunca
Better safe than sorry	Más vale precaver que tener que lamentar
Better something than nothing	Algo es algo, peor es nada
Better the devil you know than the devil you don't know	Más vale malo conocido que bueno por conocer
Between a rock and a hard place	Entre la espada y la pared
Birds of a feather flock together	Cada quien con su cada cual
By the skin of our teeth	Por los pelos
Clothes do not make the man	El hábito no hace al monje
Curiosity killed the cat	La curiosidad mató al gato
Do as I say, not as I do	Haz lo que yo digo y no lo que yo hago
Don't cry over spilled milk.	A lo hecho, pecho.

Don't look a gift horse in the mouth	A caballo regalado, no se le mira el colmillo
Don't make a mountain out of a molehill	No hay que ahogarse en un vaso de agua
Don't put off for tomorrow what can be done today	No dejes para mañana lo que puedas hacer hoy
Don't spread yourself too thin	Quien mucho abarca, poco aprieta
Easier said than done	Del dicho al hecho hay largo trecho
Enough already!	¡Basta ya!
Every cloud has a silver lining	No hay mal que por bien no venga
Give credit where credit is due	Al César lo que es del César y a Dios lo que es de Dios
Good for nothing	No sirve para nada
He who laughs last, laughs best	El que ríe último, ríe mejor
Hell is paved with good intentions	El infierno está empedrado de buenas intenciones
Honesty is the best policy	Vale más una verdad amarga que muchas mentiras dulces
I'm not buying it (take your tricks elsewhere)	A otro perro con ese hueso
If you buy cheaply, you pay dearly	Lo barato sale caro
In the blink of an eye	En un abrir y cerrar de ojos
In the short run	A corto plazo
In the wee hours of the morning	A altas horas de la madrugada
In unity there's strength	En la unión está la fuerza
It's a small world	El mundo es un pañuelo
It's better to sleep on it	Antes de hacer nada, consúltalo con la almohada
Jack of all trades, master of none	Aprendiz de todo y maestro de nada
Just around the corner	A la vuelta de la esquina
Keep your chin up	A mal tiempo buena cara
Knowledge is power	El saber no ocupa lugar
Let sleeping dogs lie	Agua que no has de beber, déjala correr
Like father, like son	De tal palo, tal astilla
Little by little the glass is filled	De gota en gota, se llena el vaso
Look before you leap	Antes que te cases, mira lo que haces
Love is blind	El amor es ciego
Misery loves company	Como el perro del hortelano, ni come ni deja comer
Money talks	Con dinero baila el perro
Nobody's perfect	Al mejor cazador se le va la liebre
Nothing is certain but death and taxes	Todo tiene solución, menos la muerte
Once bitten, twice shy	El gato escalado del agua fría huye
One good turn deserves another	Amor con amor se paga
Out of sight, out of mind	Los ojos que no ven; corazón que no siente

Out of the mouth of babes	Los niños y los locos dicen las verdades
That does it. / That's that	Ya está
The early bird catches the worm	Al que madruga Dios lo ayuda
The squeaky wheel gets the oil	Miño que no llora no mama
There's something fishy going on	Aquí hay gato encerrado
To be a labor of love	Todo sea por el amor al arte
To be a piece of cake	Ser pan comido
To be about to do something	Estar a punto de (infinitive)
To be beside oneself	Estar fuera de sí
To be dumbfounded	Quedarse boquiabierto(a)
To be finger licking good	Estar para chuparse los dedos
To be on one's way	Estar en camino
To be soaked to the skin	Estar mojado (a) hasta los huesos
To be very outspoken	No tener pelos en la lengua
To be worn out	Estar hecho polvo
To be worthwhile	Vale la pena
To bother/pester/bug	Dar la lata a (person's name)
To burn the midnight oil	Quemarse las cejas
To cost an arm and a leg	Costar un ojo de la cara
To flatter, to sweet talk	Echar flores
To get one's way	Salirse con la suya
To go from bad to worse	Ir de mal en peor
To go shopping	Ir de compras
To have nerve	Tener cara
To have sense	Tener sentido
To have your head in the clouds	Estar en las nubes
To kill two birds with one stone	Matar dos pájaros de un tiro
To laugh heartily	Reirse a carcajadas
To mess with someone	Meterse con (person's name)
To pull one's leg	Tomarle el pelo
To realize	Darse cuenta de
Too many cooks spoil the broth	Son muchas manos en un plato
Walls have ears	Las paredes oyen
We all make mistakes	Él que tiene boca se equivoca
What the eye doesn't see, the heart doesn't grieve over (ignorance is bliss)	Ojos que no ven, corazón que no siente
What's done is done	A lo hecho, pecho
When one door shuts, another opens	Donde una puerta se cierra, otra se abre
You can't teach old dogs new tricks	El loro viejo no aprende a hablar
You can't turn back the clock	El diente miente, la cana engaña, pero la arruga no ofrece nada
You drive me crazy	Me vuelves loco (a)
You reap what you sow	Quien siembra vientos recoge tempestades
You're never too old to learn	Nunca es tarde para aprender

Chapter 21: Cheat Sheets While Out And About

(Or Study Pages!)

Vocabulary Lists By Location and Theme

The Travels/Trips	Los Viajes
The airplane	El avión
The airport	El aeropuerto
The aisle / window seat	El asiento de pasillo/ de ventanilla
The arrival	La llegada
The backpack	La mochila
The baggage	El equipaje
The boarding pass	El pase de abordar
The boat	El barco / el bote
The bus	El autobús (el bús)
The camera	La cámara
The campsite	El camping
The cruise	El crucero
The customs	La aduana
The day trip	La excursión
The departure	La salida
The flight	El vuelo
The flight attendant	El / la auxiliar de vuelo
The guide	El / la guía
The historic center	El casco antiguo
The holiday	El día festivo
The hotel	El hotel
The hotel room	La habitación
The key	La llave
The lodging	El alojamiento
The one-way ticket / the rountrip ticket	El boleto de ida / el boleto de ida y vuelta
The package trip	El viaje organizado
The passport	El pasaporte
The schedule	El horario
The sleeping bag	El saco de dormir
The station (bus/train)	La estación (de autobús / de tren)
The subway	El metro
The suitcase	La maleta
The taxi	El taxi
The tourist	El/la turista
The train	El tren
The travel agency	La agencia de viajes

The travel agent	El/la agente de viajes
The trip	El viaje
The vacation	Las vacaciones
The weekend	El fin de semana
To board	Abordar
To book	Reservar
To go sightseeing	Visitar la ciudad / ver los monumentos
To pack	Hacer las maletas
To stay in a hotel	Estar alojado(a) en un hotel
To travel	Viajar

Directions/ Prepositions	Instrucciones / Preposciones
Across from	Frente a(l)
Along side of	Al lado de(l)
Along/through	Por
Around	Alrededor de(l)
Behind	Detrás de(l)
Excuse me (to get attention)	Perdón
Excuse me (when passing by someone)	Con permiso
Facing	Dar a(l)
From	De(l)
I would like ...	Me gustaría
I'm sorry	Lo siento
Near	Cerca de(l)
On top of	Encima de(l)
Over	Sobre
Straight ahead	Al derecho (or) todo recto
The address	La dirección
The alley	El callejón
The block	La cuadra (or) la manzana
The intersection	El cruce
The roundabout	La rotonda (or) la glorieta
The sign	El letrero
The street	La calle
The street corner	La esquina
The traffic light	El semáforo
To	A(l)
To change (trains)	Cambiar (de tren)
To go by (train / car / taxi)	Ir en (tren / coche / taxi)
To go for a ride	Dar una vuelta

To go on foot	Ir a pie
To the left	A la izquierda
To the right	A la derecha
To turn	Doblar
Toward	Hacia
With	Con
Within	Dentro de
Without	Sin

Business / Professional	Los Negocios / Palabras de los Negocios
Interest-free	Sin interés
The advance	Un adelanto
The advance payment	El anticipo
The balance due	El saldo deudor
The bargain	La ganga
The bill	La cuenta
The boss	El jefe / la jefa
The cash register	La caja
The cashier	El cajero / la cajera
The client / customer	El/la cliente
The closing balance	El saldo de cierre
The company	La compañía / la empresa
The credit card	La tarjeta de crédito
The employee	El empleado / la empleada
The employer	El empresorio / la empresoria
The interest rate	El tip (la tasa) de interés
The investment	La inversión
The job/employment	El empleo / el trabajo
The loan	Un préstamo
The negotiations	Las negociaciones
The outstanding balance	El saldo pendiente
The pay day	El día de paga
The percentage	El porcentage
The receipt	El recibo
The refund	El reembolso
The remainder	El resto
The sale	La liquidación
The salesperson	El/la dependiente
The statement	El extracto de cuenta
The stock	La acción
The stock market	La bolsa

The taxes	Los impuestos
The wages	La paga / el salario / el sueldo
To bargain	Regatear
To be in agreement	Estar de acuerdo
To be on sale	Estar en venta
To loan	Prestar
To make a check payable to...	Extender un cheque a favor de ...
To pay in advance	Pagar por adelantado
To pay in cash	Pagar en efectivo
To pay with a check	Pagar con checkque
To pay with a credit card	Pagar con tarjeta de crédito
To refund	Reembolsar /Devolver
To sign	Firmar

Animals and Insects	Los animales y los insectos
The ant	La hormiga
The bear	El oso
The bee	La abeja
The bird	El pájaro
The bobcat	El lince
The bull	El toro
The canary	El canario
The cat	El gato
The chipmunk	La ardilla listada
The cow	La vaca
The deer	El ciervo
The dog	El perro
The duck	El pato
The elephant	El elefante
The fish (the fish – cooked)	El pez (el pescado)
The fly	La mosca
The frog	La rana
The gecko	La lagartija
The giraffe	La jirafa
The guinea pig	El conejillo de indias
The hamster	El hámster
The hen	La gallina
The hippopotamus	El hipopótamo
The horse	El caballo
The hummingbird	El colobrí
The insect	El insecto

The lamb	El cordero
The lion	El león
The lizard	El lagarto
The monkey	El mono
The mouse	El ratón
The opossum	La zarigüeya
The ostrich	El avestruz
The parrot	El loro
The pig	El cerdo
The pigeon	La paloma
The rabbit	El conejo
The raccoon	El mapache
The rat	La rata
The rhinocerous	El rinoceronte
The rooster	El gallo
The shark	El tiburón
The sheep	La oveja
The skunk	El zorillo
The snail	El caracol
The snake	La serpiente / la culebra
The spider	La araña
The squirrel	La ardilla
The tiger	El tigre
The turtle	La tortuga

The Family	**La familia**
The brother / the sister	El hermano / la hermana
The brothers (and brothers and sisters)	Los hermanos
The children	Los hijos
The cousin	El primo / la prima
The cousins	Los primos
The dad / the mom	El papá / la mamá
The father / the mother	El padre / la madre
The father in law / the mother in law	El suegro / la suegra
The grandfather / the grandmother	El abuelo / la abuela
The grandparents	Los abuelos
The grandson / the granddaughter	El nieto / la nieta
The great grandfather/ the great grandmother	El bisabuleo / la bisabuela
The great great grandparents	Los tatarabuelos
The husband / wife	El esposo / la esposa

The nephew / the neice	El sobrino / la sobrina
The parents	Los padres
The relatives	Los parientes
The sisters	Las hermanas
The son / the daughter	El hijo / la hija
The son in law / the daughter in law	El yerno / la nuera
The stepbrother / the stepsister	El hermanastro / la hermanastra
The stepfather / the stepmother	El padrastro / la madrastra
The stepson / the stepdaughter	El hijastro / la hijastra
The uncle / the aunt	El tío / la tía

Some Useful Adjectives	Unos adjetivos útiles
Big	Grande
Blond	Rubio (a)
Boring	Aburrido (a)
Brunette	De pelo castaño
Cute	Lindo (a) / mono (a)
Dark (skin and hair)	Moreno (a)
Fat	Gordo (a)
Fun	Divertido (a)
Funny	Cómico (a)
Handsome	Guapo (a)
Long	Largo (a)
Narrow	Ancho (a)
Precious	Precioso (a)
Pretty	Bonito (a)
Short (in height)	Bajo (a)
Short (in length)	Corto (a)
Small	Pequeño (a)
Tall	Alto (a)
Thick	Grueso (a)
Thin, slender	Delgado (a)
Ugly	Feo (a)

Household Words	Palabras de la casa
The house	La casa
The lamp	La lámpara
The mirror	El espejo
The jewelry box	El estuche de joyas
The teddy bear	El osito de peluche
The chair	La silla
The armchair	El sillón
The bedspread	La sobrecama

The sheets	Las sábanas
The doll	La muñeca
The pillow	La almohada
The bed	La cama
The window	La ventana
The curtain	La cortina
The closet	El armario
The blanket	La manta
The rug	La alfombra
The floor	El suelo
The trunk	El baúl
The toy	El juguete
The nightstand	La mesa de noche
The plug	El enchufe
The dresser	La cómoda
The trashcan	El basurero
The bookshelf	El estante para libros
The sofa	El sofá
The painting	El cuadro / la pintura
The candle	La vela
The clock	El reloj
The wall	La pared
The remote control	El control remoto
The basket	La cesta
The chimney	La chimenea
The vase	El florero
The towels	Las toallas
The soap	El jabón
The toilet	El inodoro
The washcloth	El paño para lavarse
The shampoo	El champú
The bathtub	La bañera
The shower	La ducha
The sink	El fregadero
The kitchen	La cocina
The refrigerator	El refrigerador
The freezer	El congelador
The stove	La estufa
The oven	El horno
The glass (of water)	El vaso (de agua)
The fork	El tenedor
The spoon	La cuchara
The knife	El cuchillo
The napkin	La servilleta
The toaster	La tostadora

The microwave	El microonda
The dishwasher	El lavaplatos
The bucket	El balde
The lawn	El césped
The fence	La cerca
The can opener	El abrelatas
The detergent	El detergente
The bicycle	La bicicleta
The television set	El televisor
The tv	La tele
The mailbox	El buzón
The tools	Las herramientas
The drawers	Los cajones
The dining room	El comedor
The tablecloth	El mantel
The plant	La planta
The ladder	La escalera
The mouthwash	El enjuague bucal
The stereo	El estéreo
The oven mitt	El guante de horno
The bathroom sink	El lavabo
The lotion	La loción
The toilet paper	El papel higiénico
The iron	La plancha
The gate	La verja
The clothesline	El tendedero
The ruler	La regla
The door	La puerta
The washing machine	La lavadora
The dryer	La secadora
The hair dryer	El secador de pelo
The laundry room	El lavadero
The cup	La taza
The answering machine	La contestadora
The telephone	El teléfono
The fax	El fax

Chapter 22: Got It. Now What?
Ten Ideas to Keep You Talking

*There are lots of ways to practice what you've learned. Below is a list of suggestions. The final item on the list refers to the pictures on the next few pages.

1. Watch news programs (especially world news) on television. I suggest watching a half hour or so in English first, picking up on the headlines (or stories that are likely to be shown on all news programs). Then, watch the news in Spanish. Since you already are familiar with the story content, you are more likely to pick up the main ideas.

2. Watch your favorite television shows in English, but, if available, set your television to include subtitles in Spanish. Read while you watch!

3. Watch soap operas in Spanish. Many cable and television program providers offer Spanish channels with "telenovelas", or Spanish soap operas. Telenovelas differ from American soap operas in that they only last for a couple of months.

4. Watch "Destinos: An Introduction to Spanish" offered online through the Annenberg Learner Program. It was created in the 1980's and offers fifty two episodes of a telenovela developed specifically for the Spanish student.

5. Listen to Spanish music on the radio. Be patient with this process. It is a bit harder to understand the words of songs because syllables are stretched out differently in a song than they are in regular spoken language.

6. Read anything you find in Spanish! Many magazines and newspapers are available in Spanish either in hard copy or online. Read everything out loud. You and your partner can take turns reading aloud to one another.

7. Label items in your house with post-its. Identify the items out loud as you see them and/or use them during the day.

8. Keep a journal during the day. Write down at least three sentences a day that describe what you saw/did/heard/read etc. If you carry the journal with you, you can write in the present tense by saying what you see or do etc.

9. Form a Spanish Club! Find a few other friends (co-workers, neighbors, classmates) and agree to meet once or twice a month to just talk in Spanish. Before you meet, write down at least 10 questions to ask each other. Bring your journals and share some of the highlight events that you've written down over the month. Make it a Spanish Fiesta!

10. Create questions and/or stories about pictures you find in magazines. Use the next few scenes to help you get started.

VOCABULARY	QUESTIONS
La ventana – the window	
El hombre – the man	1. ¿Dónde están estas personas?
La mujer – the woman	2. ¿Qué hace la familia?
El muchacho – the boy	3. ¿Por qué limpia la casa la familia?
Barrer el piso – to sweep the floor	4. ¿Qué hay en las paredes?
Lavar – to wash	5. ¿Por qué descansa la mujer?
Limpiar – to clean	6. ¿Qué hay en el balde?
El gato – the cat	7. ¿De dónde vino el perro? ¿Está
El perro – the dog	limpio o sucio el perro?
Estar sucio – to be dirty	8. ¿Qué hace el gato?
La pintura – the painting	9. ¿Quiere el muchacho limpiar la
El florero – the flower vase	casa?
La flor – the flower	10. ¿Dónde están los muebles?
El jabón – the soap	
El balde – the bucket	
La escoba – the broom	
El polvo – the dust	
Los muebles – the furniture	
El trapo – the rag	
La pared – the wall	

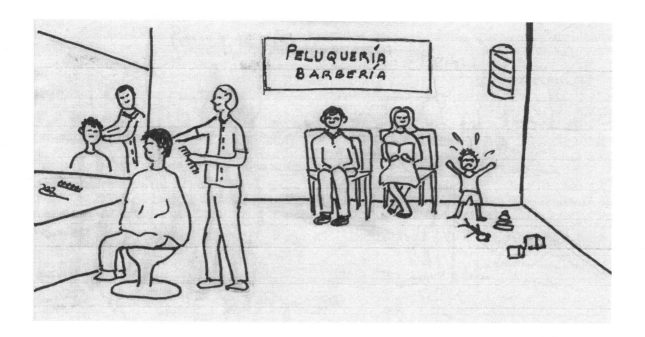

VOCABULARY	QUESTIONS
VOCABULARY La peluquería – the salon La barbería – the barber shop El peluqero – the barber El cliente – the customer El niño – the little boy El peine – the comb El cepillo – the brush El suelo – the ground/floor Esperar – to wait Los juguetes – the toys Cortar el pelo – to cut hair El espejo – the mirror El reflejo – the reflection El vestido – the dress El pelo – the hair Largo - long Corto - short El champú – the shampoo El suavizante – the conditioner La silla – the chair Estar enojado – to be angry Darle una rabieta – to throw a tantrum Leer – to read La revista – the magazine Prestar atención – to pay attention Darle una propina – to give a tip	**QUESTIONS** 1. ¿Dónde están estas personas? 2. ¿Cuántas personas esperan un corte de pelo? 3. ¿Cuántos peluqueros hay en la barbería? ¿Hay muchas o pocas personas que esperan su turno? 4. ¿Cómo está el niño? ¿Por qué se siente así? 5. ¿Quién es la mujer? ¿Le presta ella atención al niño? 6. ¿Qué hay en el suelo? ¿Por qué están aquí estas cosas? 7. ¿Usa el peluquero un peine o un cepillo? 8. ¿Le gusta al cliente su corte de pelo? ¿Cómo sabes? 9. ¿Qué lee la mujer? 10. ¿Va a darle el cliente una buena propina al peluquero?

VOCABULARY	QUESTIONS
La cocina – the kitchen	1. ¿Qué hora es? ¿Es la noche o la mañana? ¿Dónde está la familia?
El comedor – the dining room	2. ¿Qué sirve la mamá?
La mesa – the table	3. ¿Le gusta la comida al muchacho? ¿Cómo sabes?
El mantel – the tablecloth	4. ¿Qué hay en la estufa?
Estar enojado – to be mad	5. ¿Quién es la muchacha a la derecha del papá? ¿Cuántos años tiene ella?
Empujar – to push	6. ¿Es una cena formal o informal? ¿Cómo sabes?
El plato – the plate	7. ¿Qué hay en el suelo? ¿Qué hacen?
Las papas – the potatoes	8. ¿Qué beben las personas?
La leche – the milk	9. ¿Adónde van estas personas después de la cena?
El jugo – the juice	10. ¿Por qué sonríe la mujer?
El café – the coffee	
El agua – the water	
La olla – the pot	
La cacerola – the pan	
El horno – the oven	
La estufa – the stove	
La carne de res – the meat	
Las hamburguesas – the hamburgers	
El pollo – the chicken	
La hija – the daughter	
La cena – the dinner	
Sonreír – to smile	
Rogar – to beg (ruego, ruegas...)	
Dormir – to sleep (duermo, duermas...)	
Servir – to serve (sirvo, sirves...)	
El suelo – the floor	

VOCABULARY	QUESTIONS
El parque – the park	1. ¿Dónde están estas personas? ¿Qué hacen las personas?
La manta – the blanket	
La cometa – the kite	2. ¿Qué día es hoy?
To fly – volar (vuelo, vueles...)	
Andar en patineta – to skateboard	3. ¿Qué hace la mujer en la manta? ¿Por qué no juega con los otros?
El árbol – the tree	
Andar (montar) en bicicleta – to ride a bike	4. ¿Anda la persona en la bicicleta rápidamente o lentamente?
La hierba – the grass	
Las hojas – the leaves	5. ¿Qué tiempo hace hoy? ¿Qué estación del año es?
La ardilla – the squirrel	
Correr – to run	6. ¿Qué hay en el árbol? ¿Hay un nido en el árbol?
Tomar el sol – to sunbathe	
Rápidamente - quickly	7. ¿Adónde va el muchacho en la bicicleta?
Lentamente - slowly	
Hace sol – It's sunny	8. ¿Por qué corre la muchacha?
Hace buen tiempo – It's nice weather	
Hace viento – It's windy	9. ¿Se divierte mucho o poco el muchacho en la patineta?
La gorra – the hat/cap	
El tronco – the trunk (of a tree)	10. ¿Quién se divierte más? ¿Cómo sabes?
El arbusto – the bush/shrub	
Tener prisa – to be in a hurry	
Relajarse – to relax	
Ir a pie – to walk	
Las ramas – the branches	
Los shorts (pantalones cortos) – the shorts	
Divertirse – to enjoy oneself	
El nido – the nest	

VOCABULARY	QUESTIONS
El conductor – the driver	1. ¿Salpicó el conductor con agua a la señora con el perro?
Salpicar – to splash	2. ¿Por qué esperan las personas en la calle?
La calle – the street	3. ¿Se mojó el hombre en el coche?
La parada del autobús – the bus stop	4. ¿Por qué hay un letrero en la acera?
La acera – the sidewalk	5. ¿Por qué camina con el perro la señora? ¿Por qué camina en la lluvia? ¿Por qué no camina con el perro en la acera?
Mojarse – to get wet	6. ¿Adónde va el hombre en el coche?
El letrero – the sign	7. ¿Por qué tienen paraguas las personas? ¿Qué estación del año es?
El paraguas – the umbrella	8. ¿Tienen frío todas las personas?
Tener frío – to be cold	9. ¿Adónde van las dos personas en la calle?
La estación – the season	10. ¿Qué hora es? ¿A qué hora llega el autobús?

VOCABULARY
El conductor – the driver
Salpicar – to splash
La calle – the street
La parada del autobús – the bus stop
La acera – the sidewalk
Mojarse – to get wet
El letrero – the sign
El paraguas – the umbrella
Tener frío – to be cold
La estación – the season
La lluvia – the rain
El autobús – the bus
La señora – the lady
El invierno – the winter
La primavera – the spring
El verano – the summer
Llegar – to arrive
Esperar – to wait for
El charco – the puddle
Ir a pie – to walk
Las llantas – the tires
Adónde – to where
Estar enojado – to be angry
Enojarse – to get angry
La correa – the leash

QUESTIONS
1. ¿Salpicó el conductor con agua a la señora con el perro?
2. ¿Por qué esperan las personas en la calle?
3. ¿Se mojó el hombre en el coche?
4. ¿Por qué hay un letrero en la acera?
5. ¿Por qué camina con el perro la señora? ¿Por qué camina en la lluvia? ¿Por qué no camina con el perro en la acera?
6. ¿Adónde va el hombre en el coche?
7. ¿Por qué tienen paraguas las personas? ¿Qué estación del año es?
8. ¿Tienen frío todas las personas?
9. ¿Adónde van las dos personas en la calle?
10. ¿Qué hora es? ¿A qué hora llega el autobús?

APPENDIX
TRANSLATIONS AND ANSWERS

Chapter 1

Dialogue 1.1
Student A – Good morning.

Student B – Good morning. What's your name?

Student A – My name is Susan. And yours?

Student B – Pleased to meet you, Susan. My name is Carlos.

Student A – It's a pleasure, Carlos.

Student B – Likewise. See you.

Student A – Until then, Carlos.

Dialogue 1.2
Teacher: Good afternoon, Matthew. How are you?

Student: I am very well, thank you. And you? How are you?

Teacher: So-so. I have a lot of work.

Student: Then, I'll be going. I hope everything goes well with you, Ma'am.

Teacher: Thank you very much, Matthew. See you Thursday.

Dialogue 1.3
Answers may vary. Here is a sample:

Student A - Buenas noches.

Student B – Buenas noches. ¿Cómo te llamas?

Student A – Me llamo (Student A's name). ¿Y tú? ¿Cuál es tu nombre?

Student B – Mi nombres es (Student B's name).

Student A – Mucho gusto. ¿Cómo estás?

Student B – Estoy muy bien, gracias. ¿Cómo estás tú?

Student A – Estoy bien, gracias. ¿Qué hay de Nuevo?

Student B – Nada mucho.

Student A – Bueno, nos vemos el jueves.

Student B – Muy bien. Hasta el jueves. Chao.

Chapter 2

Practice 2.1:

1. Ellas
2. Él
3. Ustedes
4. Nosotros (or nosotras if you are female)

Practice 2.2

1. Son
2. Es
3. Son
4. Somos

Practice 2.3

Answers will vary.

Sample response for male:

1. Yo soy creativo, atlético, y amable.

Sample response for female:

1. Yo soy creativa, atlética, y amable

Practice 2.4

Answers will vary.

Sample response for male:

1. Yo no soy impaciente, serio, o tímido.

Sample response for female:

1. Yo no soy impaciente, seria, o tímida.

Practice 2.5

Answers will vary. See sample responses below showing both masculine and feminine endings.

1. Are you very athletic.
   Yes, I am very athletic. / No, I'm not very athletic.
   Sí, (yo) soy muy atlético (a). / No, (yo) no soy muy atlético.
2. Are you obedient or disobedient?
   I am obedient. / I am disobedient.
   (Yo) Soy obediente. / (Yo) Soy desobediente.
3. Are you very careful?
   Yes, I am very careful. / No, I'm not very careful.
   Sí, (yo) soy muy prudente. / No, (yo) no soy muy prudente.

4. Are you funny?
   Yes, I'm funny. / No, I'm not funny.
   Sí, (yo) soy cómico(a). / No, (yo) no soy cómico(a).
5. Is your spouse creative?
   Yes, my spouse is creative. / No, my spouse is not creative.
   Sí, mi esposo(a) es creativo(a). / No, mi esposo(a) no es creativo(a).
6. Is your spouse patient?
   Yes, my spouse is patient. / No, my spouse is not patient.
   Sí, mi esposo(a) es paciente. / No, mi esposo(a) no es paciente.
7. Is your brother(sister) friendly?
   Yes, my brother(sister) is friendly. / No, my brother(sister) isn't friendly.
   Sí, mi hermano(a) es amable. / No, mi hermano(a) no es amable.
8. Is your brother(sister) outgoing/extroverted?
   Yes, my brother(sister) is outgoing. / No, my brother(sister) is not outgoing.
   Sí, mi hermano(a) es extrovertido(a). / No, mi hermano(a) no es extrovertido
   (a).

Practice 2.6
Answers will vary. See sample responses below.

1. I'm a (female) teacher.
   Soy profesora.
2. My dad is a lawyer.
   Mi papá es abogado.
3. My mom is a housewife.
   Mi mamá es ama de casa.
4. My husband is a veterinarian.
   Mi esposo es veterinario.
5. My best friend is a singer.
   Mi mejor amiga es cantante.
6. My classmate is a student.
   Mi compañero de clase es estudiante.

Dialogue 2.1
Paco: Hi, Marta. How are you today?
Marta: Hi, Paco. I'm well. And you?
Paco: Very well, thank you. Marta, what are you like?
Marta: Me? I'm marvelous, Paco.
Paco: Marta, seriously. What are you like?
Marta: Well, I'm patient, energetic, and very friendly. And you, Paco? What are you
    like?
Paco: I'm athletic, energetic, and extroverted/outgoing.
Marta: And very photogenic, right?
Paco: No, I am not photogenic. And, Marta, what are your children like?
Marta: Well, my son is very serious and studious. My daughter is shy and tranquil.
Paco: Thanks, Marta.
Marta: You're welcome.

Dialogue 2.2

Student A – Hi, how are you?

Student B – Well, thank you. And you?

Student A – So-so. It was a long day. I'm a scientist. There's a lot of work. What is your profession?

Student B – I'm a banker. You are very intelligent, right? It's difficult to be a scientist.

Student A – Yes, it is difficult. Well, see you at next Thursday's class.

Student B – Very well. Until then.

Student A – Bye.

Dialogue 2.3

Student A – Good evening, (Sir/Miss/Ma'am). What is your name?

Student B – Good evening. My name is Mr./Miss/Mrs. (last name of student B).

Student A – It's a pleasure, Mr./Miss/Mrs. (last name of student B)

Student B – Likewise. And what is your name?

Student A – My name is Mr./Miss/Mrs. (last name of Student A)

Student B – What is your profession?

Student A – I am a teacher.

Student B – How interesting! You are very patient, right?

Student A – Ha ha ha… yes, I am very patient. Thank you.

Student B – I am a businessman/businesswoman and I am not very patient, but I am very pensive and careful.

Student A – You are very friendly.

Student B – Thank you. It was a pleasure (meeting you). Take care.

Student A – You too. Goodbye.

Dialogue 2.4

Student A – Hello, friend. How are you?

Student B – I'm okay. Let me introduce you to my son/daughter, (name of student C).

Student A – Nice to meet you.

Student C – The pleasure is mine.

Student A – Your son/daughter is very friendly, isn't he/she?

Student B – My son/daughter is very disobedient.

Student C – Dad/Mom, I'm not disobedient. You are impossible and too strict.

Student B – I'm not strict. I am very patient.

Student A – You two are very different, aren't you?

Student C – Yes, my dad/mom is very different from me.

Student B – My son/daughter is very intelligent, talented, and creative, but he/she is not obedient.

Student A – All families are equal. This is true. Well, good luck to you both. I'm leaving.

Student B – Bye, friend. Until next time.

Chapter 3

Practice 3.1

aduana: a/**dua**/na

casa: **ca**/sa

estudio: es/**tu**/dio

bailas: **bai**/las

colina: co/**li**/na

hablan: **ha**/blan

martes: **mar**/tes

picante: pi/**can**/te

foto: **fo**/to

tocas: **to**/cas

vecinos: ve/**ci**/nos

salsa: **sal**/sa

Practice 3.2

abril: a/**bril**

estudiar: es/tu/**diar**

pared: pa/**red**

tomar: to/**mar**

nariz: na/**riz**

voleibol: vo/lei/**bol**

ayudar: ay/u/**dar**

verdad: ver/**dad**

salud: sa/**lud**

Practice 3.3

lápiz: **lá**/piz

música: **mú**/si/ca

histórico: hi/**stó**/ri/co

marrón: ma/**rrón**

Martínez: Mar/**tí**/nez

fácil: **fá**/cil

lámpara: **lám**/pa/ra

sofá: so/**fá**

calcetín: cal/ce/**tín**

papá: pa/**pá**

mecánico: me/**cá**/ni/co

rincón: rin/**cón**

fantástico: fan/**tás**/ti/co

mamá: ma/**má**

teléfono: te/**lé**/fo/no

Practice 3.4

1. que – **ma** – do
2. e – lec- **trón**
3. ac – tua – li – **dad**
4. pan – **ta** – lla
5. al – ta – **voz**
6. es- ta – **ción**
7. ho – **gar**
8. es – **ti** – lo
9. ba – **su**- ra
10. fe – **roz**
11. va – **lien** –te
12. es – pe – **cial**
13. **to** – mas
14. es – ca – **le** – ra
15. es – **tó** – ma - go

Practice 3.5

Answers may vary. Sample complete answer responses:

1. Are you a student?
   Yes, I am a student. / No, I'm not a student.
   Sí, (yo) soy estudiante. / No, (yo) no soy estudiante.

2. Are you very serious?
   Yes, I'm very serious. / No, I'm not very serious.
   Sí, (yo) soy muy serio(a). / No (yo) no soy muy serio(a).

3. Are you from the United States?
   Yes, I'm from the United States. / No, I'm not from the United States.
   Sí, (yo) soy de los Estados Unidos. / No, (yo) no soy de los Estados Unidos.

4. Are you very creative?
   Yes, I'm very creative. / No, I'm not very creative.
   Sí, (yo) soy my creativo(a). / No, (yo) no soy muy creativo(a).

5. Is your family very athletic?
   Yes, my family is very athletic. / No, my family is not very athletic.
   Sí, mi familia es muy atlética. / No, mi familia no es muy atlética.

6. Is you family very friendly?
   Yes, my family is very friendly. / No, my family is not very friendly.
   Sí, mi familia es muy amable. / No, mi familia no es muy amable.

7. Is your spouse very patient?
   Yes, my spouse is very patient. / No, my spouse is not very patient.
   Sí, mi esposo(a) es muy paciente. / No mi esposo(a) no es muy paciente.

8. Is there a lawyer in your family?
   Yes, there is a lawyer in my family. / No, there is not a lawyer in my family.
   Sí, hay un abogado(a) en mi familia. / No, no hay un abogado(a) en mi familia.

9. Is there a teacher in your family?
   Yes, there is a teacher in my family. / No, there is not a teacher in my family.
   Sí, hay un profesor(a) en mi familia. / No, no hay un profesor(a) en mi familia.

10. Are the students in the class friendly?
    Yes, the students in the class are friendly. / No, the students in the class are not friendly.
    Sí, los estudiantes en la clase son muy amables. / No, los estudiantes en la clase no son muy amables.

11. Are you a very careful person?
    Yes, I am a very careful person. / No, I'm not a very careful person.
    Sí, (yo) soy una persona muy prudente. / No, (yo) no soy una persona muy prudente.

12. Are you a good driver?
    Yes, I am a good driver. / No, I am not a good driver.
    Sí, (yo) soy un(a) conductor(a) bueno(a). / No, (yo) no soy un(a) conductor(a) bueno(a).

13. Are you a musician?
    Yes, I'm a musician. / No, I'm not a musician.
    Sí, (yo) soy músico(a). / No, (yo) no soy músico(a).

14. Is your house very big?
    Yes, my house is very big. / No, my house is not very big.
    Sí, mi casa es muy grande. / No, mi casa no es muy grande.

15. Is your car very fast?
    Yes, my car is very fast. / No, my car is not very fast.
    Sí, mi coche es muy rápido. / No, mi coche no es muy rápido.

Chapter 4

Practice 4.1
Answers will vary. See sample responses below.

1. I like to read.
   Me gusta **leer**.
2. I like to swim.
   Me gusta **nadar**.
3. I like to watch television.
   Me gusta **mirar la televisión**.

1. I don't like to write.
   No me gusta **escribir**.
2. I don't like to skateboard.
   No me gusta **andar en patineta**.

Practice 4.2
Answers will vary. See sample responses/questions below.

1. Do you like to paint?
   ¿Te gusta **pintar**?
2. Do you like to listen to music?
   ¿Te gusta **escuchar música**?
3. Do you like to go shopping?
   ¿Te gusta **ir de compras**?
4. Do you like to paly an instrument?
   ¿Te gusta **tocar un instrumento**?
5. Do you like to skate?
   ¿Te gusta **patinar**?

Practice 4.3
Answers will vary. See sample responses/questions below.

1. Do you like surfing?
   ¿Te gusta **el surfing**?
2. Do you like hockey?
   ¿Te gusta **el hockey**?
3. Do you like water polo?
   ¿Te gusta **el esquí acuático**?

Practice 4.4
Answers will vary. See sample responses/questions below.

Student A
1. Do you like classical music?

    Yes, I like classical music. / No, I don't like classical music.

    Sí, me gusta la música clásica. / No, no me gusta la música clásica.
2. Do you like museums?

    Yes, I like museums. / No, I don't like museums.

    Sí, me gustan los museos. / No, no me gustan los museos.
3. Do you like to travel?

    Yes, I like to travel. / No, I don't like to travel.

    Sí, me gusta viajar. / No, no me gusta viajar.
4. Do you like animals?

    Yes, I like animals. / No, I don't like animals.

    Sí, me gustan los animales. / No, no me gustan los animales.
5. Do you like boxing?

    Yes, I like boxing. / No, I don't like boxing.

    Sí, me gusta el boxeo. / No, no me gusta el boxeo.

Student B
1. Do you like rock music?

    Yes, I like rock music. / No, I don't like rock music.

    Sí, me gusta la música de rock. / No, no me gusta la música de rock.
2. Do you like movies?

    Yes, I like movies. / No, I don't like movies.

    Sí, me gustan las películas. / No, no me gustan las películas.
3. Do you like to read?

    Yes, I like to read. / No, I don't like to read.

    Sí, me gusta leer. / No, no me gusta leer.
4. Do you like dogs?

    Yes, I like dogs. / No, I don't like dogs.

    Sí, me gustan los perros. / No, no me gustan los perros.
5. Do you like football?

    Yes, I like footbal. / No, I don't like football.

    Sí, me gusta el fútbol americano. / No, no me gusta el fútbol americano.

Practice 4.5
1. No le gustan las verduras.
2. No nos gusta la playa.
3. No les gusta cantar.
4. ¿Les gusta el fútbol?
5. Le gustan los fines de semana.

6. Le gusta la música.

Practice 4.6
1. A Tomás le gusta nadar.
2. A él le gusta jugar al baloncesto.
3. ¿A Ud. le gusta viajar?
4. A mis amigos les gusta leer.
5. ¡A mi esposo le gusta cocinar, pero a mí me gusta comer!

Practice 4.7
Answers may vary. Sample responses are provided below.

1. What do you love?
   I love to ice skate.
   Me encanta patinar sobre hielo.
2. What fascinates you?
   Different cultures fascinate me.
   Las culturas diferentes me fascinan.
3. What interests you?
   Movies are interesting to me. (I'm interested in movies)
   Las películas me interesan.
4. What bothers you?
   Traffic bothers me.
   El tráfico me molesta.

Practice 4.8
Answers vary. See Practice 4.7 for ideas on how to respond.

Practice 4.9
Answers will vary. See the sample responses below.

1. Does art interst you?
   Yes, art interests me. / No, art doesn't interest me.
   Sí, el arte me interesa. / No, el arte no me interesa.
2. Are you interested in museums?
   Yes, I'm interested in museums. / No, I'm not interested in museums.
   Sí, me interesan los museos. / No, no me interesan los museos.
3. Do you like reading or writing more? (What do you like more – to read or to write?)
   I like reading more. / I like writing more.
   Me gusta más leer. / Me gusta más escribir.
4. Do little kids bother you?
   Yes, little kids bother me. / No, little kids don't bother me.
   Sí, los niños me molestan. / No, los niños no me molestan.

5. Do animals bother you?
   Yes, animals bother me. / No, animals don't bother me.
   Sí, los animales me molestan. / No, los animales no me molestan.
6. Do you like traveling much?
   Yes, I like traveling a lot. / No, I don't like traveling much.
   Sí, me gusta viajar mucho. / No, no me gusta viajar mucho.
7. How do you like to travel? In plane, in train, by car or by foot?
   I like to travel by ... plane, train, car, by foot.
   Me gusta viajar ... en avión, en tren, en carro, a pie.
8. What do you like to do on weekends?
   I like to go shopping on weekends.
   Me gusta ir de compras los fines de semana.

Practice 4.10

Estudiante A – Hola, (name of partner). ¿Cómo estás?

Estudiante B – Hola, (name of partner). Estoy bien, gracias. ¿Qué pasa?

Estudiante A – Nada mucho. ¿(Name of partner), te interesa el arte?

Estudiante B – ¡Sí, el arte me fascina! Me gusta mucho.

Estudiante A – Bueno, en el Museo Norton Simon hay una pintura de Diego Rivera. ¿Te

gustan las pinturas de Diego Rivera?

Estudiante B – ¡Sí, me encantan!

Dialogue 4.1 – La primera cita (the first date)

Tomás – Hi Marta. How are you?

Marta - I'm well, Tomás, thank you. And thank you for inviting me to this restaurant.

Tomás – It's a pleasure, Marta. I would like to get to know you better.

Marta – Likewise, Tomás.

Tomás – Well then. What do you like to do in your free time?

Marta - ¡Uf! A lot! I really like to read and to spend time with friends. I don't like to draw, but I'm interested in art. I like to listen to music – Oh! And I love to play sports! But I don't like to watch sports. And you, Tomás? What do you like to do?

Tomás – I like sports also. But I like to watch sports on tv. I like to cook and I like cooking shows.

Marta - Are you interested in history programs? *I* love them.

Tomás - Yes, I like history a lot. But the history programs bother me. They are very boring. I prefer to read history from historical books.

Marta – You are very interesting, Tomás. We have a lot in common.

Dialogue 4.2 – Vecinos nuevos (New Neighbors)

Neighbor #1 – Good morning. I'm your new neighbor, Marisa. Pleased to meet you.

Neighbor #2 – Pleased to meet you, Marisa. My name is Alisa. Welcome to the neighborhood.

Neighbor #1 – Thanks, Alisa. Tell me...do you have a family?

Neighbor #2 – Yes, there are my husband, my three children, and myself. And two dogs, too. And you? Do you have family?

Neighbor #1 – Yes, in my house there are my husband, my two kids, and myself. And one very disagreeable cat. I don't like the cat, but my kids love it.

Neighbor #2 – Ha, ha, ha. My kids love every kind of animal. What are your kids interested in? Do they like video games?

Neighbor #1 – Yes, they're fascinated with them. But I don't like them. For them, I prefer sports. They like to play sports and it's healthier. Don't you think?

Neighbor #2 – Of course. My whole family likes sports too. And you? Do you like to read? There's a reading club where we talk once in a while about contemporary books. Are you interested in a club like this?

Neighbor #1 – Yes, I'm very interested. I love to read.

Neighbor #2 – How great!

Chapter 5

Practice 5.1

1. **Los** vestidos
2. **Las** camisas
3. **La** chaqueta
4. **Las** camisetas
5. **las** gafas de sol
6. **Las** blusas
7. **El** sombrero
8. **Los** zapatos
9. **El** anillo
10. **La** bolsa

Practice 5.2

1. unos vestidos
2. unas camisas
3. una chaqueta
4. una blusa
5. un sombrero
6. unos zapatos
7. una camiseta
8. unos anillos
9. una bolsa
10. unas gafas de sol

Practice 5.3

1. the lamp
2. the bed
3. the telephone
4. the outlet/plug
5. the bathtub / the shower
6. the hair dryer
7. the thermostat
8. the arm chair and the ottoman
9. the washing machine
10. the dryer
11. the alarm clock
12. the trash can and the trash
13. the painting
14. the television set
15. the sofa/couch
16. the light bulb

Practice 5.4

1. What is this? Is it the telephone?
   No, it's not the telephone. It's the alarm clock.
   No, no es el teléfono. Es el despertador.
2. What is this? Is it the bed?
   No, it's not the bed. It's a chair and ottoman.
   No, no es la cama. Es el sillón y el otomano.
3. What is this? Is it the outlet/plug?
   No, it's not the outlet. It's the thermostat.
   No, no es el enchufe. Es el termostato

4. What is this? Is it the hair dryer?

   No, it's not the hair dryer. It's the (clothes) dryer.

   No, no es el secador de pelo. Es la secadora.

5. What are these? Is it the trash can and the trash?

   No, it's not the trash can and the trash. It's the bathtub and shower.

   No, no es el basurero y la basura. El la bañera y la ducha.

6. What is this? Is it the television set?

   Yes, it's the television set.

   Sí, es el televisor.

Practice 5.5

1. a theater
2. a post office
3. a car
4. a parking lot
5. a bank
6. an ATM
7. a police station
8. a restaurant
9. a train station
10. a bus
11. a store
12. a building
13. a highway
14. a (street) corner
15. a gas station
16. a hotel

Practice 5.6

1. Is it a restaurant?

   No, it's not a restaurant. It's a post office.

   No, no es un restaurante. Es un correo.

2. Is it a building?

   Yes, it's a building.

   Sí, es un edificio.

3. Is it a highway?

   Yes, it's a highway.

   Sí, es una carretera.

4. Is it a parking lot?

   No, it's not a parking lot. It's a bus.

   No, no es un estacionamiento. Es un autobús.

5. Is it a gas station?

   Yes, it's a gas station.

   Sí, es una estación de gasolina.

6. Are they some cars?

   Yes, they are some cars.

   Sí, son unos carros.

Practice 5.7

1. a fork
2. a chair
3. a napkin and a fork
4. the bottle of wine
5. a knife
6. a table
7. a spoon
8. the food
9. a glass
10. the bathroom/restroom
11. a cup
12. the bill
13. the plate
14. the waiter
15. the menu
16. the waitress

Practice 5.8

1 . What is this?

It's a menu.

Es un menú.

2. Who is this? Is it the professor?

No, it's not the professor. It's the waitress.

No, no es la profesora. Es la camarera.

3. What are these?

It's a fork and a napkin.

Es un tenedor y una servilleta.

4. What is this?

It's a glass.

Es un vaso.

5. What is this?

It's a bottle of wine.

Es una botella de vino.

6. What is this?

It's a knife.

Es un cuchillo.

Chapter 6

Practice 6.1
1. If you like to wear the color black, are you a funny or serious person?
    - If I like to wear the color black, I am a (funny/serious) person.
    - Si me gusta llevar el color negro, soy una persona (cómica/seria).
2. If you like to wear the color green, are you a patient or impatient person?
    - If I like to wear the color green, I am a (patient/impatient) person.
    - Si me gusta llevar el color verde, soy una persona (paciente/impaciente).
3. If your favorite color is red, are you extroverted or introverted?
    - If my favorite color is red, I am (extroverted/introverted).
    - Si mi color favoirto es rojo, soy (extrovertido(a)/introvertido(a)).
4. What color is your house?
    - My house is (white, blue, gray, etc.)
    - Mi casa es (blanca, azul, gris, etc.)
5. What color is your kitchen?
    - My kitchen is (yellow, green, orange, etc.)
    - Mi cocina es (amarilla, verde, anaranjada, etc.)
6. What color is your bedroom?
    - My bedroom is (blue, red, black, etc.)
    - Mi dormitorio es (azul, rojo, negro, etc.)
7. What color is your car?
    - My car is (red, black, etc.)
    - Mi carro es (rojo, negro, etc.)
8. What color are your eyes?
    - My eyes are (blue, green, brown)
    - Mis ojos son azules, verdes, marrones)
9. What color are your shoes?
    - My shoes are (white, black, blue, etc.)
    - Mis zapatos son (blancos, negros, azules, etc.)
10. What is your favorite color?
    - My favorite color is (green, blue, pink, etc.)
    - Mi color favorito es (verde, azul, rosado, etc.)

Practice 6.2
1. Ella es alta.
2. Él es guapo.
3. (Nosotros) somos trabajadores.
4. El libro es largo.
5. La película es corta.
6. (Yo) soy bajo(a).

7. Los perros son gordos.

8. Las blusas son bonitas.

9. Las chicas son jóvenes.

10. Las chaquetas nuevas son feas.

Practice 6.3

1. El perro se llama Buster.
2. El perro es perezoso.
3. El perro es blanco.
4. Es un perro inteligente.
5. A las familias les gusta el perro.

Practice 6.4

Answers will vary. See sample descriptions below.

1. Emocionante, fácil, aburrido, etc.

2. Bonita, larga, agradable, etc.

3. Divertida, fácil, larga, etc.

4. Nuevos, bonitos, grandes, etc.

5. Bonito, emocionante, agradable, etc.

6. Aburridas, divertidas, cortas, etc.

7. Amables, inteligentes, trabajadores, etc.

Chapter 7

Practice 7.1
1. su *(It's her cousin.)*
2. mi *(I prepare my project before going to work.)*
3. sus *(They are their books.)*
4. tu *(It's your milk.)*
5. sus *(They are her nephews from New York.)*
6. nuestros *(Our uncles are from Mexico).*
7. sus *(Their shirts are red).*
8. vuestras *(All of your boots are big.)*
9. sus *(His shoes are black.)*
10. mis *(These are my sheets of paper.)*
11. nuestra *(It is our motorcycle.)*
12. su *(She is not his sister.)*
13. sus *(They are your dogs.)*
14. su *(The pretty woman is their mom.)*
15. nuestro *(Our orange juice is here.)*

Dialogue 7.1
Student A – Hi (partner's first name). How are you?

Student B – I'm very well, thank you. And you?

Student A – I'm fantastic. Listen, I really like horror films. Do you like them too?

Student B – Well, yes... more or less, yes.

Student A - Perfect! There's a phenomenal movie in the theater on Friday. Do you want to go with me?

Student B – Yes! Of course!

Student A – How great! I'll see you on Friday!

Student B – Until then.

Dialogue 7.2
Student A – Hi. What is your name?

Student B – My name is (Student B's name). And you?

Student A – I am (Student A's name). What do you like to do?

Student B – I really like to ride a bike in the mountains and also I like to play tennis.

Student A – How interesting! I like to ride a bike too, but I don't like tennis much. I am a terrible tennis player.

Student B – Ah, yes... but you are a very active person, right? What do you like to do in your free time?

Student A – Well, I like to go shopping in the store Nordstrom and I like to spend time with friends. I also like to exercise in the gym.

Student B – Do you like museums?

Student A – Oh, yes, I love them!

Student B – Do you want to go with me to the museum tonight? It's a museum of modern art.

Student A – I'm sorry, but I can't. I have work tonight. Maybe another day.

Student B – Very well. Maybe Saturday.

Student A – On Saturday? Yes, excellent. We'll see each other then?

Student B – Yes, until then, (Student A's name).

Dialogue 7.3

Student A – Good morning, Mr/Mrs.. (Student B' last name). How are you?

Student B – Good morning (Student A's first name). I'm very well, thank you. How are you?

Student A – I'm well, Mr./Mrs. (Student B's last name) Thank you. Mr./Mrs. Student B's last name), what do you like to do in your free time?

Student B – Well, (Student A's first name), I like many activities. I like to read and to practice sports. I like to use the computer and to write.

Student A - What sports do you like most?

Student B – Let's see… I like football and basketball.

Student A - ¿And what do you like to write?

Student B – I like to write romantic poems.

Student A – Romantic poems? How great! Are you very romantic?

Student B – No, I'm not very romantic, but I like delicious meals.

Student A – Delicious meals?

Student B – Yes, I write poems for my husband/wife and he/she likes my romantic poems. When he/she receives my romantic poem, he/she prepares me a delicious meal.

Dialogue 7.4

Student A – Hi, (Student B's name).

Student B – Hi, (Student A's name). How are you?

Student A – Well, thank you. Hey, (Student B's name), what is this?

Student B – It's a building. It's my apartment.

Student A – Your apartment? The building is big, isn't it?

Student B – Yes, but my apartment is small.

Student A – And, who is the woman?

Student B – The woman is my sister, Julia.

Student A – I like her purple pants.

Student B – Yeah? I don't like them. They're ugly.

Student A – Who is the man with her?

Student B – The man is my dad.

Student A – Ah. He is very tall and slender. He is also very young, isn't he?

Student B – Yes, he is young.

Student A – And the dog? Is it your dog?

Student B – No, it isn't my dog. It's my sister's dog. It is a very fat and lazy dog. I
don't like it.

Student A – Don't you like animals?

Student B – Yes, generally I like animals, but her dog isn't my favorite. Besides, I like
cats more. They are more tranquil. Dogs are more active.

Student A – I like dogs better.

Student B – Well, to each his own.

Student A – Yes, that's true, friend, that is true. Well, we'll see each other soon, eh?

Student B – Yes, (Student A's first name). Bye.

Dialogue 7.5

Student A – Hi, (Student B's first name). I like your (color of Student B's shirt) shirt. Is
it new?

Student B – Yes, it's new. Thank you very much.

Student A – And I like your (descriptive word and another item of clothing your partner
is wearing. Is it/Are they new too?

Student B – Oh, no! It is/They are old.

Student A – What color are your eyes? Green?

Student B – My eyes are (color of Student B's eyes: azules, marrones, verdes)

Student A – Your eyes are pretty with your shirt.

Student B – Thank you very much, (Student A's first name).

Student A – You're welcome.

Dialogue 7.6

Student A – Good morning, Sir/Ma'am. Can I help you?

Student B – Yes, of course.

Student A – I need a new sweater.

Student B – What color?

Student A – A brown or black sweater.

Student B – In the women's department, there are very pretty sweaters.

Student A – Thank you.

Student B – No problem.

Chapter 8

Practice 8.1
1. 641
2. 534
3. 7,211
4. 3,700,014
5. 11,415
6. 9,353

Practice 8.2
1. How much does the book cost? (15)

   The book costs 15 dollars.

   El libro cuesta quince dólares.
2. How many students are in the class? (27)

   There are 27 students in the class.

   Hay veinte y siete (veintisiete) estudiantes en la clase.
3. How many clocks are there in the class? (1)

   There is 1 (a) clock in the class.

   Hay un reloj en la clase.

Practice 8.3
1. cuatrocientos cincuenta y cinco
2. cuarenta y nueve
3. ochenta y siete
4. dos mil trescientos sesenta y uno
5. seis mil setecientos dos
6. ochocientos quince
7. nueve mil seiscientos once
8. mil doscientos trece
9. ciento veinte y tres
10. quinientos noventa y siete

Practice 8. 4
You're on your own! (Answers will vary depending upon the numbers your partner chooses!)

Practice 8.5

Answers will vary. As samples, here are three years that are significant to the author of the book.

Year (in number)	Year written
1987	Mil novecientos ochenta y siete
2001	Dos mil uno
2012	Dos mil doce

Chapter 9

Practice 9.1

1. What day is today?

   Today is (Monday, Tuesday, Wednesday, Thursday, Friday, Saturday, Sunday)

   Hoy es (lunes, martes, miércoles, jueves, viernes, sábado, domingo).

2. If today is Tuesday, what day is tomorrow?

   If today is Tuesday, tomorrow is Wednesday.

   Si hoy es martes, mañana es miércoles.

3. If yesterday was Sunday, what day is today?

   If yesterday was Sunday, today is Monday.

   Si ayer fue domingo, hoy es lunes.

4. Today is Friday. What day was yesterday?

   Yesterday was Thursday.

   Ayer fue jueves.

5. What is your favorite day of the week?

   My favorite day of the week is (Monday, Tuesday, Wednesday, Thursday, Friday, Saturday, Sunday)

   Mi día favorito de la semana es (lunes, martes, miércoles, jueves, viernes, sábado, domingo).

Practice 9.2

1. In what month is your birthday?

   My birthday is in (January, Febrary, March, April, May, June, July, August, September, October, November, December)

   Mi cumpleaños es en (enero, febrero, marzo, abril, mayo, junio, julio, agosto, septiembre, octubre, noviembre, diciembre)

2. In which month is Thanksgiving?

   In November.

   En noviembre.

3. In which month is St. Patrick's Day?

   In March.

   En marzo.

4. In which month is the Independence Day of the U.S.?

   In July.

   En julio.

5. In which month is the first day of summer?

   In June.

   En junio.

6. In which month is April Fool's Day?

    In April.

    En abril.

    *Note: In parts of Latin America, it's on December 28!

7. In which month is Christmas?

    In December.

    En diciembre.

8. In which month is Valentine's Day?

    In February.

    En febrero.

9. In which month is the first day of the year?

    In January.

    En enero.

10. In which months do classes in school generally begin?

    In September or August.

    En septiembre o agosto.

Practice 9.3
Answers will vary.

Practice 9.4
1. Son las cuatro.
2. Son las diez y cuarto. (or, informally) Son las diez y quince.
3. Son las seis y media.
4. Es la una menos cinco. (or, informally) Son las dos y cincuenta y cinco.
5. Son las diez menos veinte y cinco (veinticinco). (or, informally) Son las nueve y treinta y cinco.
6. Son las nueve y diez y seis (dieciséis).
7. Es la una menos diez. (or, informally) Son las doce y cincuenta.
8. Es la una y diez.
9. Son las tres y veinte y cinco (veinticinco).
10. Son las seis menos cuatro. (or, informally) Son las cinco y cincuenta y seis.
11. Es mediodía.
12. Son las cinco de la mañana.

Practice 9.5
1. What time does the bus arrive?

    The bus arrives at 1:15.

    El autobús llega a la una y cuarto. (or, informally) El autobús llega a la una y quince.

2. At what time is the party?

    The party is at 8:00PM.

    La fiesta es a las ocho de la noche.

3. What time does the movie begin?

    The movie begins at 10:00 sharp.

    La película empieza a las diez en punto.

4. What time does the museum open?

    The museum opens at 9:30 AM.

    El museo abre a las nueve y media de la mañana.

5. At what time does the train leave?

    The train leaves at 2:45 PM.

    El tren sale a las tres menos cuarto de la tarde. (or, informally) El tren sale a las dos y cuarenta y cinco de la tarde.

Practice 9.6

1. La fiesta es a las once.
2. La clase es a la una menos cuarto. (or, informally) La clase es a las doce y cuarenta y cinco.
3. El tren llega a las siete menos diez. (or, informally) El tren llega a las seis y cincuenta.
4. El restaurante se abre a las ocho y veinte y cinco (veinticinco).
5. La función es a las cinco y cuarto. (or, informally) La función es a las cinco y quince.

Dialogue 9.1

Student: Excuse me, Professor, but what is the date today?

Professor: Today is February 14.

Student: February 14th? You don't say!

Professor: Why do you say that?

Student: The 14th of February is Valentine's Day, right?

Professor: Ah, yes, ... that it is. Is it an important day for you?

Student: No, but it's an important day for you.

Professor: Why do you say that?

Student: Because your husband(wife) is there at the door with flowers for you.

Dialogue 9.2

Husband: Happy anniversary, my dear!

Wife: Thanks, my love. I also believe that every day is an anniversary for us.

Husband: I have a surprise for youy. At 6:00 tonight, to celebrate our anniversary, we are going to eat in "Luxurious House" – the most elegant restaurant of the center of the city. I have reservations for the two of us.

Wife: Seriously? At Luxurious House? But that restaurant costs an arm and a leg. And it isn't...

Husband: Well, that's how it is, my dear. Only the best for you. And that isn't all. At 8:00, we are going to the new musical in the theater. I have reserved seats. It's fantastic! Don't you think so?

Wife: Yes, my love, but ...

Husband: There are no buts! That's how we are going to celebrate.

Wife: Well, my love.... But, when is our anniversary?

Husband: It's today!

Wife: What is the date today?

Husband: It's July 12th, right?

Wife: Yes, my love. It is July 12th. But our anniversary is the 12th of August.

Husband: ¡Oh, geeze!

Wife: Don't worry, my love. There is no problem. We will celebrate our anniversary with an elegant dinner and a new musical on the 12th of July AND the 12th of August! What a good idea! Don't you think?

Chapter 10

Practice 10.1
Answers will vary. See sample responses below.

1. What is the weather like in Fall?

   It's cool in the Fall.

   Hace fresco en el otoño.

2. Does it rain a lot in April?

   No, it doesn't rain a lot in April.

   No, no llueve mucho en abril.

3. Do you like the rain?

   Yes, I like the rain. / No, I don't like the rain.

   Sí, me gusta la lluvia. / No, no me gusta la lluvia.

4. Does it snow here in our city?

   Yes, it snows here in our city. / No, it doesn't snow here in our city.

   Sí, nieva aquí en nuestra ciudad. / No, no nieva aquí en nuestra ciudad.

5. What's the weather like in California?

   It's good weather in California. It's hot and sunny.

   Hace buen tiempo en California. Hace calor y sol.

6. What do you like to wear in the winter?

   I like to wear sweaters and coats in the winter.

   Me gusta llevar los suéteres y los abrigos en el invierno.

7. Do you wear a sweater or a bathing suit when it's cold?

   I wear a sweater when it's cold.

   Llevo un suéter cuando hace frío.

8. Do you wear a sweater or a t-shirt when it's cool out?

   I wear a sweater when it's cool out.

   Llevo un suéter cuando hace fresco.

9. Do you wear a scarf or a t-shirt when it's hot?

   I wear a t-shirt when it's hot.

   Llevo una camiseta cuando hace calor.

10. Do you wear a raincoat when it rains?

   Yes, I wear a raincoat when it rains.

   ¿Lleva un impermeable cuando llueve?

Practice 10.2
There is a woman named Marisol. (What is the name of the woman? Marta or Marisol? – *Marisol*) **Marisol is going to go to a party tonight at 8:00.** (Where is Marisol going – to a class or to a party? – *to a party*) **Marisol is very excited because she likes parties.** (Is Marisol angry or excited? - *emocionada*) (Does Marisol like or not like parties? – *le gustan las fiestas*) **She is also excited because she**

really like a man whose name is Diego and Diego is going to be at the party also. *(Does Marisol like or not like Diego? – le gusta mucho) (Is Diego going to be at the party – yes or no? – Sí)* **But Marisol has a problem. She doesn't know what to wear to the party.** *(What problem does Marisol have? – not having money or not knowing what to wear? – no sabe qué llevar)* **It is very cold but she doesn't want to wear a sweater and pants. She prefers to wear a short dress without sleeves.** *(Does Marisol prefer to wear pants or a dress? –un vestido)* **But it's snowing and it's very cold.** *(Is it hot or is it cold? – Hace frío)* **She decides to wear a short red dress with a sweater and some high heels.** *(Does she decide to wear pants or the dress? – el vestido)*

Marisol arrives to the party at 8:30. *(Does Marisol arrive on time to the party or a little late? – un poco tarde)* **Marisol sees Diego immediately. Diego is wearing jeans, boots, and a coat. Everyone at the party is wearing clothing for winter.** *(Are the people at the party wearing clothing for winter or for summer? – para el invierno)* **There is one other person that is wearing a short dress also. It's a tall woman with long, brown hair** *(Is the tall woman wearing pants or a dress? – un vestido)* **The woman arrives to the side of Diego and gives him a kiss. Marisol realizes that Diego has a girlfriend.** *(Does Diego have a girlfriend – yes or no? – sí)* **At this moment, Marisol is cold and she wants her pants and sweater.** *(Is Marisol happy in her dress? – No)*

Chapter 11

Practice 11.1

Infinitive	English	Stem
hablar	to speak, to talk	*habl*
ayudar a	To help	ayud
buscar	To search, look for	busc
contestar	To answer	contest
Desear	To desire, to want	desea

Practice 11.2

Estudiar-to study

Yo	estudio	Nosotros Nosotras	estudiamos
Tú	estudias	Vosotros Vosotras	estudiáis
Él Ella Usted	estudia	Ellos Ellas Ustedes	estudian

Practice 11.3
1. Habla
   The girl talks with friends.
2. Sacan
   The students take out the books from the backpacks.
3. Llegáis
   Are you guys arriving by bus?
4. Llevamos
   Carlos and I are wearing suits to work.
5. Enseña
   The teacher teaches the lesson.
6. Toman
   David and Juan are taking a Spanish class.

7. Estudian

   You all always study a lot.

8. Miras

   Do you watch a lot of television?

9. Escucho

   I listen to the radio in the afternoon.

10. Entran

    The students enter in the classroom at 7:00 sharp.

11. Estudian

    Maria and you study for the Spanish class.

12. Escuchan

    The good students listen to the teacher.

13. Participan

    The bad students don't participate in the class.

14. Llevo

    I always carry a pen and some sheets of paper in my backpack.

15. Pasan

    Many of my friends spend vacations in the mountains.

Practice 11.4

1. (Yo) necesito un lápiz.
2. Ella desea unos libros.
3. (Nosotros) hablamos español.
4. Ellos charlan con sus amigos.
5. ¿Escuchas la música?

Practice 11.5

Answers may vary. See sample responses below.

1. Do you speak French or English?

   I speak English.

   (Yo) hablo inglés.

2. Does your husband/wife help?

   Yes, my husband helps. / No, my husband doesn't help.

   Sí mi esposo ayuda. / No, mi esposo no ayuda.

3. What program do you watch on television?

   I watch the news on television.

   (Yo) miro los noticieros en la televisión.

4. Are you looking for a dictionary?

   Yes, I'm looking for a dictionary. / No, I'm not looking for a dictionary.

   Sí, (yo) busco un diccionario. / No, (yo) no busco un diccionario.

5. Do you wear jeans to work?

   Yes, I wear jeans to work. / No, I don't wear jeans to work.

   Sí, (yo) llevo los jeans al trabajo. / No, (yo) no llevo los jeans al trabajo.

6. Do you spend much time with your family?

Yes, I spend a lot of time with my family. / No, I don't spend much time with my family.

Sí, (yo) paso mucho tiempo con mi familia. / No, (yo) no paso mucho tiempo con mi familia.

Practice 11. 6

Infinitive	English	Stem
comer	To eat	*com*
beber	To drink	beb
leer	To read	le
vender	To sell	vend

Practice 11.7

Leer = to read

Yo	**leo**	Nosotros Nosotras	**leemos**
Tú	**lees**	Vosotros Vosotras	**leéis**
Él Ella Usted	**lee**	Ellos Ellas Ustedes	**leen**

Practice 11.8

1. lee

   She reads many romantic books.

2. aprenden

   The Spanish students learn a lot in the class.

   la clase.

3. creo

   I believe that Spanish is easy.

4. corremos

   You and I run in the evenings/nights.

5. vendes

   Do you sell old books here?

Practice 11.9

Answers will vary. See sample responses below.

1. Do you believe in ghosts?

    Yes, I believe in ghosts. / No, I don't believe in ghosts.

    Sí, (yo) creo en los fantasmas. / No, (yo) no creo en los fantasmas.

2. Do you eat in expensive restaurants?

    Yes, I eat in expensive restaurants. / No, I don't eat in expensive restaurants.

    Sí, (yo) como en los restaurantes caros. / No, (yo) no como en los restaurantes caros.

3. Does your family eat in fast food restaurants?

    Yes, my family eats in fast food restaurants. / No, my family doesn't eat in fast food restaurants.

    Sí, mi familia come en los restaurantes rápidos. / No, mi familia no come en los restaurantes rápidos.

4. Do your friends understand Spanish?

    Yes, my friends understand Spanish. / No, my friends don't understand Spanish.

    Sí, mis amigos comprenden el español. / No, mis amigos no comprended el español.

5. Do you drink red wine?

    Yes, I drink red wine. / No, I don't drink red wine.

    Sí, (yo) bebo el vino rojo. / No, (yo) no bebo el vino rojo.

Práctica 11.10

1. (Yo) veo el perro grande.
2. ¿Ves muchas películas?

Practice 11.11

Infinitive	English	Stem
vivir	To live	*viv*
abrir	To open	abr
compartir	To share	compart
escribir	To write	escrib
recibir	To receive	recib

Practice 11.12

abrir-to open

Yo		Nosotros Nosotras	
	abro		**abrimos**
Tú		Vosotros Vosotras	
	abres		**abrís**
Él Ella Usted	**abre**	Ellos Ellas Ustedes	**abren**

Practice 11.13

1. recibimos

    We receive many gifts on birthdays.

2. viven

    Juan and you live in the city of Glendale.

3. comparten

    My parents share the car.

4. suben

    José y Juana go up/climb the stairs in order to arrive to the third story.

5. escribe

    Paula writes an article for the newspaper.

6. abren

    You all open the books in the Spanish class.

Practice 11.14

Spanish translations are provided first. Since answers given may vary when asking each other the questions, sample answers are provided for the second part of the exercise.

1. ¿Escribes los poemas?

    Yes, I write poems. / No, I don't write poems.

    Sí, (yo) escribo los poemas. / No, (yo) no escribo los poemas.

2. ¿Recibes muchas llamadas telefónicas?

    Yes, I receive many telephone calls. / No I don't receive many telephone calls.

    Sí, (yo) recibo muchas llamadas telefónicas. / No, (yo) no recibo muchas llamadas telefónicas.

3. ¿Compartes tu casa con otra persona?

    Yes, I share my house with another person. / No, I don't share my house with another person.

    Sí, (yo) comparto mi casa con otra persona. / No, (yo) no comparto mi casa con otra persona.

4. ¿Compartes tu carro/coche con otra persona?

Yes, I share my car with another person. / No, I don't share my car with another person.

5. Sí, (yo) comparto mi carro/coche con otra persona. / No, (yo) no comparto mi carro/coche con otra persona.

6. ¿Asistes a otras clases?

Yes, I attend other classes. / No, I don't attend other classes.

Sí, (yo) asisto a otras clases. / No, (yo) no asisto a otras clases.

Practice 11.15

Student A

1. Do you understand this lesson?

Yes, I understand this lesson. / No, I don't understand this lesson.

Sí, (yo) comprendo esta lección. / No, (yo) no comprendo esta lección.

2. Do you chat with friends on the computer?

Yes, I chat with friends on the computer. / No, I don't chat with friends on the computer.

Sí, (yo) charlo con amigos por computadora. / No, (yo) no charlo con amigos por computadora.

3. Do you live in a big or small house?

I live in a big house. / I live in a small house.

(Yo) vivo en una casa grande. / (Yo) vivo en una casa pequeña.

4. Do you work in an office or en your house?

I work in an office. / I work in my house.

(Yo) trabajo en una oficina. / (Yo) trabajo en mi casa.

5. Do you learn quickly or slowly?

I learn quickly. / I learn slowly.

(Yo) aprendo rápidamente. / (Yo) aprendo lentamente.

Student B

1. Do you read mystery novels?

Yes, I read mystery novels. / No, I don't read mystery novels.

Sí, (yo) leo novelas de misterio. / No, (yo) no leo novelas de misterio.

2. Do you travel to different countries?

Yes, I travel to different countries. / No, I don't travel to different countries.

Sí, (yo) viajo a países diferentes. / No, (yo) no viajo a países diferentes.

3. Do you attend many parties.

Yes, I attend many parties. / No, I don't attend many parties.

Sí, (yo) asisto a muchas fiestas. / No, (yo) no asisto a muchas fiestas.

4. Do you play an instrument?

Yes, I play an instrument. / No, I don't play an instrument.

Sí, (yo) toco un instrumento. / No, (yo) no toco un instrumento.

5. Do you watch many films/movies?

Yes, I watch many films/movies. / No, I don't watch many films/movies.

Sí, (yo) miro muchas películas. / No, (yo) no miro muchas películas.

Practice 11.16

Answers will vary. Below are sample complete sentence answers.

1. Do you chat with your friends in class?

   Yes, I chat with my friends in class. / No, I don't chat with my friends in class.

   Sí, (yo) charlo con mis amigos en clase. / No, (yo) no charlo con mis amigos en clase.

2. Do you fix cars?

   Yes, I fix cars. / No, I don't fix cars.

   Sí, (yo) arreglo coches. / No, (yo) no arreglo coches.

3. Do you call your friends on the phone every night?

   Yes, I call my friends on the phone every night. / No, I don't call my friends on the phone every night.

   Sí, (yo) llamo a mis amigos por teléfono cada noche. / No, (yo) no llamo a mis amigos por teléfono cada noche.

4. Do you drink a lot of milk?

   Yes, I drink a lot of milk. / No, I don't drink a lot of milk.

   Sí, (yo) bebo mucha leche. / No, (yo) no bebo mucha leche.

5. Do you read romantic novels?

   Yes, I read romantic novels. / No, I don't read romantic novels.

   Sí, (yo) leo novelas románticas. / No, (yo) no leo novelas románticas.

6. Do you read mystery novels?

   Yes, I read mystery novels. / No, I don't read mystery novels.

   Sí, (yo) leo novelas de misterio. / No, (yo) no leo novelas de misterio.

7. Do you believe in ghosts?

   Yes, I believe in ghosts. / No, I don't believe in ghosts.

   Sí, (yo) creo en los fantasmas. / No, (yo) no creo en los fantasmas.

8. Do your friends read a lot?

   Yes, my friends read a lot. / No, my friends don't read a lot.

   Sí, mis amigos leen mucho. / No, mis amigos no leen mucho.

9. Do you see many movies in the movie theater?

   Yes, I see many movies in the movie theater. / No, I don't see many movies in the movie theater.

   Sí, (yo) veo muchas películas en el cine. / No, (yo) no veo muchas películas en el cine.

10. Do you write poems?

    Yes, I write poems. / No, I don't write poems.

    Sí, (yo) escribo poemas. No, (yo) no escribo poemas.

11. Do you receive many letters from your boyfriend/girlfriend?

    Yes, I receive many letters from my boyfriend/girlfriend. / No, I don't receive many letters from my boyfriend/girlfriend.

    Sí, (yo) recibo muchas cartas de mi novio(novia). / No, (yo) no recibo muchas cartas de mi novio (novia).

12. Do you attend many meetings?

    Yes, I attend many meetings. / No, I don't attend many meetings.

    Sí, (yo) asisto a muchas reuniones. / No, (yo) no asisto a muchas reuniones.

13. Do you need a lot of attention?

    Yes, I need a lot of attention. / No, I don't need a lot of attention.

    Sí, (yo) necesito mucha atención. / No, (yo) no necesito mucha atención.

14. Do you eat dinner with your family every night?
    Yes, I eat dinner with my family every night. / No, I don't eat dinner with my family every night.
    Sí, (yo) ceno con mi familia cada noche. / No, (yo) no ceno con mi familia cada noche.
15. Do you buy a lot of expensive clothing?
    Yes, I buy a lot of expensive clothing. / No, I don't buy a lot of expensive clothing.
    Sí, (yo) compro mucha ropa cara. / No, (yo) no compro mucha ropa cara.
16. Do you wash the dishes after eating?
    Yes, I wash the dishes after eating. / No, I don't wash the dishes after eating.
    Sí, (yo) lavo los platos después de comer. / No, (yo) no lavo los platos después de comer.
17. Do you watch a lot of television?
    Yes, I watch a lot of television. / No, I don't watch a lot of television.
    Sí, (yo) miro mucha televisión. / No, (yo) no miro mucha televisión.
18. Do you use the computer a lot?
    Yes, I use the computer a lot. / No, I don't use the computer a lot.
    Sí, (yo) uso mucho la computadora. / No, (yo) no uso mucho la computadora.
19. Do you study in your bed?
    Yes, I study in my bed. / No, I don't study in my bed.
    Sí, (yo) studio en mi cama. / No, (yo) no studio en mi cama.
20. Do you want to live in a big house?
    Yes, I want to live in a big house. / No, I don't want to live in a big house.
    Sí, (yo) deseo vivir en una casa grande. / No, (yo) no deseo vivr en una casa grande.
21. Do you live in an elegant apartment?
    Yes, I live in an elegant apartment. / No, I don't live in an elegant apartment.
    Sí, (yo) vivo en un apartamento elegante. / No, (yo) no vivo en un apartamento elegante.
22. Do you take many photos?
    Yes, I take many photos. / No, I don't take many photos.
    Sí, (yo) saco muchas fotos. / No, (yo) no saco muchas fotos.
23. Do you listen to music in Spanish?
    Yes, I listen to music in Spanish. / No, I don't listen to music in Spanish.
    Sí, (yo) escucho música en español. / No, (yo) no escucho música en español.
24. Do you listen to the radio in the car?
    Yes, I listen to the radio in the car. / No, I don't listen to the radio in the car.
    Sí, (yo) escucho el radio en el coche. / No, (yo) no escucho el radio en el coche.
25. Do you learn quickly?
    Yes, I learn quickly. / No, I don't learn quickly.
    Sí, (yo) aprendo rápidamente. / No, (yo) no aprendo rápidamente.
26. Do you like to climb mountains?
    Yes, I like to climb mountains. / No, I don't like to climb mountains.
    Sí, me gusta subir las montañas. / No, no me gusta subir las montañas.

Dialogue 11.1

Carla - What are you looking for, Marta?

Marta - Me? I am looking for an interesting place to visit this weened. My friend, Jorge, arrives on Saturday.

Carla – What do you want to do?

Marta – Jorge likes museums a lot. I want to go to an art museum.

Carla – My neighbor works in the Getty Museum. He organizes the visits of tourists and it's an interesting and beautiful museum.

Marta – That's a fantastic idea, Carla. I'll call your neighbor today. Thank you very much.

Dialogue 11.2

Susana – What do you do on the weekends, Carlos?

Carlos – On weekends? I study my Spanish lessons, I talk with friends, I watch tv, and sometimes I dance in the evenings. And you, Susana?

Susana – On Fridays I eat dinner with my family in a fabulous restaurant. On Saturdays I chat with friends and I clean my house.

Carlos – And on Sundays?

Susana – On Sundays? After cleaning my house, I rest!

Dialogue 11.3

Student A – Hi friend, … how are you?

Student B – I'm well, friend. Very well. And you?

Student A – Well, well… thank you. Hey, what is the date today?

Student B – Well, today is the 17th of March. It's St. Patrick's Day. Why?

Student A – I don't like to gossip, but our friend – the teacher – is drinking green beer now.

Student B - Really? I believe it's to celebrate St. Patrick's Day. Don't you think?

Student A – I think so, but I also think that we shouldn't talk more about this. The teacher shouldn't drink drink beer in class.

Student B – Well, I do agree.

Dialogue 11.4

Student A – Good morning, Sir/Maam. Are you using the computer here?

Student B – Good morning. Yes, I am using it. Do you want to use the computer?

Student A – Yes, I am looking for information on the internet.

Student B – Well, I will finish within a few minutes. Doyou want to wait a little bit?

Student A – No, I don't want to wait. I'll look for another computer. Thank you.

Student B – You're welcome.

Dialogue 11.5

Student A – Hi, Mom. What are you preparing for dinner?

Student B – I'm preparing some tamales with meat and rice with chicken.

Student A – Fantastic. And when do we eat dinner?

Student B – At 6:00 sharp, son. You should wash your hands right now.

Student A – Good, Mom. Are we watching a movie while we eat dinner? I want to see a program on tv.

Student B – No, my son, no. We talk about our days while we eat dinner. We don't want to watch a program while we eat. It isn't healthy to watch tv and eat at the same time.

Student A – You are the most boring mom of all.

Student B – Poor little thing... but that's life.

Dialogue 11.6

Student A – Good morning, my dear.

Student B – Good morning, my love.

Student A – Do you want to climb a mountain today?

Student B – Climb a mountain? No, my love. I don't want to climb a mountain. Do you want to go shopping?

Student A – Of course not, my dear. There isn't enough money to to shopping with you. How about we watch the baseball game between the Dodgers and the Giants?

Student B – Ay, my love. No. OH, I know ... how about we skate hand in hand along the beach?

Student A – My dear, I don't skate well. Uh, I know ... how about we swim in the water of the ocean?

Student B - Me? Wear a bathing suit in front of everyone? No. Well, how about we dance to the music here in the house? How romantic! Don't you think?

Student A – Yes, it's very romantic. But ... no. I don't dance well either.

Student B – My love, I want to do something today. How about we eat something?

Student A – That's a fantastic idea, my dear. What are you preparing to eat?

Chapter 12

Practice 12.1
Answers will vary. See sample responses below.

1. I watch television every day.
   (Yo) miro la televisión cada día.
2. I never write poems.
   (Yo) nunca escribo poemas.
3. I always cook at home.
   (Yo) siempre cocino en casa
4. I use the computer every day.
   (Yo) uso la computadora todos los días.
5. Once in a while I take a class.
   (Yo) tomo una clase de vez en cuando.
6. I rarely buy new clothing.
   Rara vez compro ropa nueva.
7. I speak often with my parents.
   Hablo mucho con mis padres.
8. I always practice Spanish
   (Yo) siempre practico el español. (¡Claro que sí! ☺)

Practice 12.2
Answers will vary. See sample responses below.

1. How often do you read the newspaper?
   I read the newspaper *often*.
   (Yo) leo el periódico *a menudo*.
2. How often do you walk with your dog?
   I walk with my dog *once in a while*.
   (Yo) camino con mi perro *de vez en cuando*.
3. How often do you listen to music?
   I listen to music *every day*.
   (Yo) escucho música *todos los días*.
4. How often do you rest during the day?
   I *never ever* rest during the day.
   (Yo) *jamás* descanso durante el día.
5. How often do you travel?
   I *rarely* travel.
   (Yo) *rara vez* viajo.
6. How often do you use a dictionary?
   I *rarely* use a dictionary.
   (Yo) uso un diccionario *rara vez*.

7. How often do you play an instrument?

I play an instrument *often*.

(Yo) toco un instrumento *a menudo*.

8. How often do you clean the house?

I clean the house *every weekend*.

(Yo) limpio la casa *cada fin de semana*.

9. How often do you see your relatives?

I see my relatives *once in a while*.

(Yo) veo a mis parientes *de vez en cuando*.

10. How often do you walk to the supermarket?

I never walk to the supermarket.

(Yo) nunca camino al supermercado.

Chapter 13

Practice 13.1

    1.¿Quiénes hablan español? *(Who speaks Spanish?)*

      ¿Qué hablan tus padres? *(What do your parents speak?)*

    2. ¿Cuántos libros hay en la clase? *(How many books are there in the class?)*

      ¿Qué hay en la clase? *(What is there in the class?)*

      ¿Dónde están los cinco libros? (*Where are the five books?)*

    3. ¿Qué es el libro? *(What is the book?)*

    4. ¿Quién descansa en su cuarto? *(Who rests in his/her room?)*

      ¿Dónde descansa Luisa? *(Where does Luisa rest?)*

      ¿Qué hace Luisa? *(What is Luisa doing?)*

    5. ¿Cuándo estudias? (*When do you study?)*

      ¿Quién estudia por la mañana? *(Who studies in the morning?)*

    6. ¿Cómo es Jorge? *(What is Jorge like?)*

      ¿Dónde vive Jorge? *(Where does Jorge live?)*

      ¿Dónde está el apartamento? *(Where is the apartment?)*

Practice 13.2

    1. ¿Dónde está el parque?

    2. ¿Quién lee el libro?

    3. ¿Adónde vas?

    4. ¿Cuánto cuesta el collar?

    5. ¿Cuántas camas hay en el cuarto?

    6. ¿Por qué estudias el español?

Dialogue 13.1

Father/Mother: Son/Daughter, you need your shoes. Where are they?

Son/Daughter:　They are in the garage. But, why do I need my shoes?

Father/Mother:　You need your shoes because we are going to the supermarket.

Son/Daughter　And why are we going to the supermarket?

Father/Mother:　We are going to the supermarket because we need food.

Son/Daughter　Why do we need food from the supermarket? Why don't we go to the restaurant to buy food?

Father/Mother: We don't go to the restaurant because it costs too much money to buy food in the restaurants.

Son/Daughter　Why does food from the restaurants cost so much?

Father/Mother:　It costs a lot of money because we pay for the service and for the chefs that prepare the meal for us.

Son/Daughter　Why do we pay for the service?

Father/Mother:　We pay for the service because ... oh, son/daughter... I don't know. Put on your shoes and let's go.

Dialogue 13.2

The employer:	Good morning. Sit down, please.
The applicant:	Good morning. Thank you.
The employer:	You would like to work for us. Right?
The applicant:	Yes. I would like to be a salesperson here. M
The employer:	Good. I have some questions for you. First, what is your address?
The applicant:	I live on 2365 Sierra Vista Street in Los Angeles, California.
The employer:	Okay. And how do you spell your last name?
The applicant:	My last name is Bengoa. B-E-N-G-O-A.
The employer:	And, what experience do you have in being a salesperson?
The applicant:	I've been a salesperson in the story "Jewels" for three years. I sell rings with diamonds, silver bracelets, golden earrings, and much more. There are many people that like jewels.
The employer:	Yes, I believe it! And how much money do you receive each month from your job now?
The applicant:	Wow! A lot! Almost 5,000 every month. It's incredible.
The employer:	5,000 dollars? Okay, Sir/Maam, I don't understand. Why do you want to be a salesperson here? You are not going to earn as much money here.
The applicant:	Why? The answer is easy, Sir/Maam. In the store where I work, I work a lot because there are many customers. Here in your store there aren't as many customers and I am not going to work as much. In my opinion, it's more important to rest and enjoy life than to work. Don't you think?

Chapter 14

Practice 14.1
Answers will vary. See sample sentences below.

1. Estoy *curioso* (a).
   I'm *curious*. (feeling curious)
2. Estoy *avergonzado* (a).
   I'm *embarrassed*.
3. Estoy *emocionado* (a).
   I'm *excited*.

Practice 14.2
Answers will vary. See sample sentences below.

1. No estoy *desanimado(a)*.
   I'm not *discouraged*.
2. No estoy *de mal humor*.
   I'm not *in a bad mood*.
3. No estoy *apático(a)*.
   I'm not *apathetic*.

Practice 14.3
1. Are you very tired tonight?
   No, I'm not tired tonight. I'm worried.
   No, no estoy cansad(a) esta noche. Estoy preocupado(a).
2. Do you feel very discouraged with the class?
   No, I don't feel very discouraged with the class. I feel sure of myself.
   No, no me siento muy desanimado(a) con la clase. Me siento seguro(a) de mí mismo(a).
3. Is the professor very silly?
   Yes, the professor is very silly.
   Sí, la profesora está muy loca.
4. Does your classmated feel very anxious?
   No, my classmate doesn't feel very anxious. He/She feels distracted.
   No, mi compañero(a) de clase no se siente muy ansioso. Mi compañero de clase se siente distraído(a).
5. Is your son mischievous?
   No, my son isn't mischievous. He is curious.
   No, mi hijo se está travieso. Está curioso.
6. Are you very stressed tonight?
   No, I'm not very stressed tonight. I'm excited.
   No, no estoy muy estresado esta noche. Estoy emocionado(a).

Practice 14.4

1. (Yo) tengo frío.
2. Ella tiene hambre.
3. (Nosotros) tenemos mucho sueño.
4. Ellos tienen que comer.
5. (Yo) tengo que ir.
6. Él tiene ganas de bailar.
7. Ella tiene treinta y cinco años.
8. (Yo) tengo (your age?) años.
9. ¿Tienes (tú) sed?
10. ¿Tiene miedo ella?

Practice 14.5

Answers may vary. Suggestion provided below.

1. You just arrived to class and there is a very difficult exam. How are you?
   Estoy nervioso(a) y ansioso(a). *(I'm nervous and anxious.)*
2. You just used an incorrect word in Spanish and everyone is laughing at you. How are you feeling?
   Me siento avergonzado(a). *(I feel embarrassed.)*
3. You are on the beach. It's cool, but it's not cold and you don't have to do anything. How do you feel?
   Me siento feliz. Me siento contento(a). Estoy de buen humor. *(I feel happy. I feel content. I'm in a good mood.)*
4. You just won the lottery. How do you feel?
   Me siento feliz. Estoy en las nubes. *(I feel happy. I'm on cloud nine.)*
5. You just arrived home after a long day at work. How are you?
   Tengo sueño. *(I am sleepy.)*
6. Your friend says that two plus two is five and you say that dos plus two is four. What do you have?
   Tengo razón. *(I'm right.)*
7. You are in the desert and you just walked for miles. How are you and what do you have?
   Estoy cansado(a) y tengo sed. (I'm tired and I'm thirsty.)
8. You are in the office and there are many papers on your desk. The telephone is ringing and there is an urgent email that you have to write. How are you at this moment?
   Estoy ansioso(a) y ocupado(a). *(I'm anxious and I'm busy.)*
9. It's two in the morning and your are in your house in your bed. There is a sound on the patio. You see a figure that is running by the window. How do you feel?
   Tengo miedo. Estoy nervioso(a). *(I am scared. I am nervous.)*

10. You have an appointment with the doctor at 3:30. It is 3:15 now. You are in your ar and there is a lot of traffic. How are you? What do you have?
Estoy ansioso(a). Tengo prisa. (I'm anxious. I'm in a hurry.)

Practice 14.6
Translate the following sentences to Spanish.

1. Me duele el brazo.
2. Me duelen las piernas.
3. ¿Te duelen las rodillas?
4. Me duele la cabeza.
5. Le duele el pulgar.
6. Le duelen los dedos del pie.
7. ¿Qué le duele?
8. Le duele el estómago.

Dialogue 14.1
Student A – Why are you sad?
Student B – It's not that I am sad. I'm very tired today. I don't feel well.
Student A – Why are you so tired?
Student B – It's that I don't like when it's very hot like it is today. I feel very tired and my head hurts.
Student A – Oh, yes, I understand you. My head hurts too when it's so very hot out. But I like the sun. Hey, friend, are you thirsty? Do you want to drink a soda in that restaurant?
Student B – I'm not thirsty, but I'm hungry. Yes, I'll go with you to the restaurant to eat and have a drink with you. Thank you.
Student A – Don't mention it. Let's go.

Dialogue 14.2
Doctor – Good morning, Maam. How are you today? Why are you here to see me?
Patient – Good morning, Doctor. I'm here because my throat hurts and I don't feel well.
Doctor - Do you have a fever?
Patient – No, Doctor. I don't have a fever.
Doctor – Good. I believe that you speak too much and for that reason your throat hurths. Don't talk anymore and you are going to get better.
Patient – But, Doctor. I'm a teacher. I have to talk a lot in the class to teach the students. Not talk? Well, that's not possible for me. Isn't there any other remedy?
Doctor – Of course, Maam. There's another remedy. You only have to change your profession.

Patient - Change my profession? Wow, what craziness! I'm finished here. You are a charlatan. I'm leaving.

Doctor – Okay, Maam, but you have to pay before leaving. The advice from a doctor like me doesn't come without a price. Goodbye and take care.

Dialogue 14.3

Son(Daughter) – Mom, Mom.

Mother – What's happening, son? What do you have? Does something hurt?

Son(Daughter) – No, Mom, nothing hurts me.

Mother – Do you have a fever?

Son(Daughter) – No, Mom, I don't have a fever.

Mother – Are you thirsty? I have milk, juice, water...

Son(Daughter) – No, Mom. I'm not thirsty. It's that ...

Mother – You're hungry, right? Well, there are ham sandwiches, fruit ...

Son(Daughter) – No. I'm not hungry. Es It's that ...

Mother - Are you cold, hot, sleepy ...? Tell me son, what do you have?

Son(Daughter) – Mom, nothing hurts me, I don't have a fever, I'm not hot, cold hungry or sleepy. It's that I'm very lucky and I feel like telling you that you are the best mom of all.

Chapter 15

Dialogue 15.1

Anita: Verónica, why are you smiling?

Verónica: I'm smilying because I'm thinking about my trip that I'm going to take next week.

Anita: How great! Where are you going to travel to?

Verónica: On Friday I'm going to travel to San Diego. There, I'm going to visit my little sister. We are going to eat in a Mexican restaurant there.

Anita: Delicious! And afterwards? What are you going to do?

Verónica: My little sister and I are going to take a cruise through Mexico.

Anita: How exciting! Now I'm jealous. I want to take a cruise through Mexico!

Verónica: Ha, ha. Next time maybe.

Practice 15.1

1. Ellos van a nadar a las dos.
2. ¿Qué vas a hacer hoy?
3. ¿Va a ir él al banco?
4. ¿Vamos a visitar el museo?
5. Voy al parque.

Practice 15.2:

Answers will vary. See sample responses below.

1. Where are you going tomorrow at noon?

   I'm going to have lunch tomorrow at noon.

   Voy a almorzar mañana al mediodía.

2. What are you going to do after class?

   I'm going to go to my house after class.

   Voy a ir a mi casa después de clase.

3. What are you going to do this weekend?

   ¿Qué vas a hacer este fin de semana?

4. What are you going to do to celebrate your birthday?

   I'm going to have a party to celebrate my birthday.

   Voy a dar una fiesta para celebrar mi cumpleaños.

Chapter 16

Practice 16.1
Answers will vary. Below are sample responses.

1. Do you know how to play the piano?

   Yes, I know how to play the piano. / No, I don't know how to play the piano.

   Sí, (yo) sé tocar el piano. / No, (yo) no sé tocar el piano.

2. Do you give money to the banker?

   Yes, I give money to the banker. / No, I don't give money to the banker.

   Sí, (yo) doy el dinero al banquero. / No, (yo) no doy el dinero al banquero.

3. Do you thank your parents?

   Yes, I thank my parents. / No, I don't thank my parents.

   Sí, (yo) agradezco a mis padres. / No, (yo) no agradezco a mis padres.

4. Do you see/watch television a lot?

   Yes, I see/watch television a lot. / No, I don't see/watch television a lot.

   Sí, (yo) veo la televisión mucho. / No, (yo) no veo la televisión mucho.

5. Do you go out with your friends?

   Yes, I go out with my friends. / No, I don't go out with my friends.

   Sí, (yo) salgo con mis amigos. / No, (yo) no salgo con mis amigos.

Practice 16.2
Answers will vary. See sample responses below.

Student A
1. At what time doyou leave class?

   I leave class at 9:00PM.

   Salgo de la clase a las nueve de la noche.

2. Do you recognize people easily?

   Yes, I recognize people easily. / No, I don't recognize people easily.

   Sí, (yo) reconozco fácilmente a las personas. / No, (yo) no reconozco fácilmente a las personas.

3. What do you know how to do very well?

   I know how to skate very well.

   (Yo) sé patinar bien.

Student B
1. What do you do on weekends?

   I spend time with friends on weekends.

   (Yo) paso tiempo con amigos los fines de semana.

2. What do you bring to a party?

   I bring a salad to a party.

   (Yo) traigo ensalada a una fiesta.

3.Do you see your relatives often?

Yes, I see my relatives often. / No, I don't see my relatives often.

Sí, (yo) veo a mis parientes mucho. / No, (yo) no veo a mis parientes mucho.

Practice 16.3

1. dorm
2. pet
3. tend
4. pod
5. reg

Practice 16.4

1. (Yo) caliento el agua.
2. (Nosotros) calentamos la piscina.
3. ¿Prefieres (tú) el café o el té?
4. (Nosotros) nunca mentimos.
5. (Yo) quiero ir al museo, pero (vosotros) queries ir al cine.
6. ¿A qué hora empieza/comienza la película?
7. ¿Qué piensan Uds.?
8. ¿En qué piensas (tú)?
9. Ellos siempre pierden.
10. (Nosotros) cerramos las ventanas cuando hace frío.

Practice 16.5

Juanita gets up at 6:00 in the morning. (Does Juanita get up at 6:00 or at 7:00? *Juanita se despierta a las seis.*) Juanita wants to go to the beach because it's hot out.. (Where does Juanita want to go? *A la playa.*) **Juanita thinks a lot about the things she wants to take.** (Does Juanita think about her husband or in the things she wants to take to the beach? *En las cosas que quere llevar a la playa.*) **Juanita thinks about taking a beach chair but prefers to take a towel.** (Does Juanita prefer to bring a beach chair or a towel?). **Juanita begins to prepare her lunch.** (Does Juanita begin to prepare a snack or her lunch? *Su almuerzo.*) **Juanita wants a ham sandwich and fruit for her lunch. She puts bread, hame and grapes in a cooler.** (Does she put the meal in a basket or in a cooler? *En una neverita.*) **Juanita looks for the keys to her car, but she doesn't see them.** (Does Juanita see her keys or not? *No*). **Juanita feels sad because she can't go to the beach today without the keys to her car.** (Does Juanita feel sad or happy? *Triste.*) **Finally, Juanita sees her backpack on the sofa. In her backpay are the keys to her car.** (Are the keys to her car in the sofa or in the backpack? *En la mochila*). **Juanita feels happy because she is going to go the beach today.** (Is Juanita going to go to the beach? *Sí.*)

Practice 16.6

1. (Yo) me acuesto temprano, pero ellos se acuestan tarde.
2. ¿Hueles (tú) el café?
3. (Nosotros) volvemos mañana.
4. ¿Cuánto cuestan las camisas?
5. ¡(Yo) puedo hablar español ahora!
6. Ella no recuerda mi nombre.
7. Llueve y truena.
8. (Nosotros) dormimos bien cuando hace frío.
9. (Yo) no puedo encontrar mis llaves.
10. ¿Mueves (tú) los libros a la mesa?

Practice 16.7

Marta always dreams about traveling to Puerto Vallarta. (What does Marta dream about? Traveling to Puerto Vallarta or to Acapulco? *A Puerto Vallarta*) **She loves the beach and the Mexican culture.** (Does she love the Mexican or Puerto Rican culture? *La cultura mexicana.*) **But she can't travel to Puerto Vallarta because it costs a lot of money and she doesn't have a lot of money.** (Does Marta have a lot or a little money? *Tiene poco dinero.*) **It's that Marta doesn't have work now.** (Does Marta have work? *No.*)

One day, Marta has lunch in a taco restaurant and she sees her friend, Susana. (Does Marta see her mom or her friend? *Su amiga.*) **Susana shows Marta a photo of her new house.** (What is there in the photo? *La casa nueva de Susana.*) **Her new house is in Puerto Vallarta!** (Where is the new house? *En Puerta Vallarta.*)

"I want to find a person to take care of my house while I'm not there," says Susana. Susan needs help with her house. (Does Susana need a person to help in the house or to visit the house? *Necesita una persona para ayudar.*)

"I can help in your house," Marta tells her. Marta feels very happy and excited because Susan likes the idea very much. (Does Marta have a job now? *Sí.*)

Practice 16. 8

1. (Yo) me despido de mis amigos.
2. ¿Sirve la comida el mozo?
3. Mis amigos se ríen del chiste.
4. ¿Sigues (tú) las reglas?
5. ¿Quién sigue?
6. (Nosotros) pedimos pizza y refrescos(sodas).
7. (Yo) me visto a las seis de la mañana.
8. Los estudiantes repiten las palabras con la maestro(profesora).
9. We smile when we see our friends..
10. (Yo) compito en muchos deportes.

Practice 16.9

Answers will vary. Translations provided below to help you choose appropriate information.

1. You compete in (many / few) sports.
2. Generally, you serve meals with (a lot of meat / many vegetables).
3. You (never / always / once in a while) order a glass of wine with your meal.
4. Generally you take (a lot of / little) time to get dressed in the morning.
5. You smile (a lot / little).
6. When a party ends, generally you (say goodbye / don't say goodbye) to your friends.
7. You measure (twice / only once) before making something or building something.
8. You (always / sometimes / never) follow the rules.
9. You sleep (less than / more than) eight hours every night.
10. (You can / You can't) play an instrument.
11. You (always / once in a while / never) hang up your clothes in the closet.
12. You go to bed (late / early).
13. You wake up (early / late).
14. You (remember / don't remember) a lot about your childhood.
15. Generally you eat lunch (at home / in a resataurant).
16. (You close, You open) the windows when you are in the house during the day.
17. You enjoy yourself (a lot / a little) en parties where there are many people.
18. (You like / You don't like) when it snows.
19. (You like / You don't like) when it rains.
20. You prefer the color (red / green / yellow / black / orange / white / blue).

Chapter 17

Practice 17.1

Infinitive	"Yo" form of verb	Ud. command form	Uds. command Form
1. comer (eat)	*Como*	*Coma*	*Coman*
2. escuchar (listen)	Escucho	Escuche	Escuchen
3. sentar(se) (sit)	Siento	Siéntese	Siéntense
4. abrir (open)	Abro	Abre	Abren
5. decir (say, tell)	Digo	Diga	Digan
6. leer (read)	Leo	Lea	Lean
7. correr (run)	Corro	Corra	Corran
8. beber (drink)	Bebo	Beba	Beban
9. parar (stop)	Paro	Pare	Paren
10. doblar (turn)	Doblo	Doble	Doblen
11. tomar (take)	Tomo	Tome	Tomen
12. mirar (watch)	Miro	Mire	Miren
13. llamar (call)	Llamo	Llame	Llamen
14. quitar(se) (take off)	Quito	Quítese	Quítense
15. lavar(se) (wash)	Lavo	Lávese	Lávense

Practice 17. 2

Infinitive	"Yo" form of verb	Ud. command form	Uds. command Form
1. llegar (arrive)	*Llego*	*Llegue*	*lleguen*
2. buscar (look for)	Busco	Busque	Busqen

3. almorzar (have lunch)	Almuerzo	Almuerce	Almuercen
4. pagar (pay)	Pago	Pague	Paguen
5. tocar (play, an instrument)	Toco	Toque	Toquen
6. comenzar (begin)	Comienzo	Comience	Comiencen

Practice 17.3
1. ¡No corra!
2. Pague la cuenta.
3. No venda la casa.
4. Doble a la derecha.
5. Siéntese y abra el libro.
6. No duerma ahora.

Practice 17.4
1. No vayan al museo.
2. No dé el dinero al mozo(camarero).
3. Miren la película.
4. Doblen a la izquierda.
5. No estén tristes.
6. Acuéstense temprano.

Práctica 17.5
Answers may vary.

1. Doctor, I'm always tired. I don't have much energy during the day. I sleep four to six hours each night. Sometimes I do exercise.
   Coma bien. Coma muchas verduras. Beba mucha agua. Duerma más de ocho o nueve horas cada noche. Haga más ejercicio. *(Eat well. Eat a lot of vegetables. Dring a lot of water. Sleep more than 8 to 9 hours each night. Do more exercise.)*
2. Doctor, my stomach hurts a lot. I eat three meals every day and I drink a lot of milk. I like cheese a lot and I love eggs, and for that reason I eat a lot of cheese and eggs.
   No coma tanto queso. No tome leche. Coma más verduras. Haga ejercicio cada día. *(Don't eat so much cheese. Don't drink milk. Eat more vegetables. Do exercise every day.)*

3. Doctor, I feel very anxious all the time. I can't concentrate because I'm very nervous. At least I can do my work, and I work six days each week and each day I work nine or ten hours. I don't see my friends or my family a lot, but I like my work a lot and I'm happy in the office where I work.

   Descanse más. No haga tanto trabajo sin un descanso. Haga ejercicio. *(Rest more. Don't do so much work without a break. Exercise.)*

4. Doctor, I feel horrible. My eyes hurt, my head hurts and I sneeze all day. My throat hurts and I'm very sleepy.

   Descanse. Tome una aspirina y mucha agua. *(Rest. Take an aspirin and drink a lot of water.)*

Práctica 17. 6
You're on your own on this one! See if your partner performs the commands you give!

Chapter 18

Practice 18.1
1. Imperfect
2. Preterite
3. Imperfect
4. Imperfect
5. Preterite
6. Imperfect

Practice 18.2
1. miraba
2. hablaba
3. trabajaban
4. cantábamos
5. escuchabas
6. viajaba
7. trabajabais
8. almorzabas
9. gustaba
10. pensaba

Practice 18.3
1. Vivía
2. escribía
3. comprendían
4. recibíamos
5. sabías
6. leían
7. creíais
8. repetías
9. vendía
10. abríamos

Practice 18.4
1. (Yo) era alto(a).
2. Ella iba a la playa los fines de semana.
3. Ellos veían el perro.
4. Era la una.
5. Eran las seis y media.
6. Íbamos al parque.
7. ¿Eras bajo(a)?
8. (Yo) siempre veía la casa verde.

9. Mi mamá era muy activa en la escuela.

10. ¿Iban al cine cada fin de semana?

Practice 18.5
Answers may vary. See samples to help you with structure and translations.

When you were ten years old....

1. Were you living in California?

   Yes, I was living in California. / No, I wasn't living in California.

   Sí, (yo) vivía en California. / No, (yo) no vivía en California.

2. Did you drink milk?

   Yes, I used to drink milk. / No I didn't drink milk.

   Sí, (yo) bebía leche. / No, (yo) no bebía leche.

3. Did you listen to classical music?

   Yes, I listened to classical music. / No, I didn't listen to classical music.

   Sí, (yo) escuchaba la música clásica. / No, (yo) no escuchaba la música clásica.

4. Did you like to read?

   Yes, I liked to read. / No, I didn't like to read.

   Sí, me gustaba leer. / No, no me gustaba leer.

5. Did you obey your parents?

   Yes, I obeyed my parents. / No, I didn't obey my parents.

   Sí, (yo) obedecía a mis padres. / No, (yo) no obedecía a mis padres.

6. Did you see many movies in the movie theater? /

   Yes, I saw many movies in the movie theater. / No, I didn't see many movies in the movie theater.

   Sí, (yo) veía muchas películas en el cine. / No, (yo) no veía muchas películas en el cine.

7. Were you big or small for your age?

   I was (big) (small) for my age.

   (Yo) era (grande) (pequeño/a) para mi edad.

8. Did you like to color with crayons?

   Yes, I liked to color with crayons. / No, I didn't like to color with crayons.

   Sí, me gustaba colorear con crayones. / No, no me gustaba colorear con crayones.

9. Did you visit the park a lot?

   Yes, I visited the park a lot. / No, I didn't visit the park a lot.

   Sí, (yo) visitaba mucho el parque. / No, (yo) no visitaba mucho al parque.

10. Did you know how to ride a bicycle?

    Yes, I knew how to ride a bicycle. / No, I didn't know how to ride a bicycle.

    Sí, (yo) sabía montar en bicicleta. / No, (yo) no sabía montar en bicicleta.

11. Did you go to the museums once in a while?

    Yes, I went to the museums once in a while. / No, I didn't go to the museums once in a while.

    Sí, (yo) iba a los museos de vez en cuando. / No, (yo) no iba a los museos de vez en cuando.

12. Did you play with friends?

Yes, I played with friends. / No, I didn't play with friends.

Sí, (yo) jugaba con amigos. / No, (yo) no jugaba con amigos.

13. Did you play an instrument?

Yes, I played an instrument. / No, I didn't play an instrument.

Sí, (yo) tocaba un instrumento. / No, (yo) no tocaba un instrumento.

14. Did you travel a lot?

Yes, I traveled a lot. / No, I didn't travel a lot.

Sí, (yo) viajaba mucho. / No, (yo) no viajaba mucho.

15. Did you move a lot?

Yes, I moved a lot. / No, I didn't move a lot.

Sí, (yo) me mudaba mucho. / No, (yo) no me mudaba mucho.

16. Were you shy?

Yes, I was shy. / No, I wasn't shy.

Sí, yo era tímido(a). / No, (yo) no era tímido(a).

17. Did you camp in a tent?

Yes, I camped in a tent. / No, I didn't camp in a tent.

Sí, (yo) acampaba en una tienda de acampar. / No, (yo) no acampaba en una tienda de acampar.

18. Did you visit your grandparents?

Yes, I visited my grandparents. / No, I didn't visit my grandparents.

Sí, (yo) visitaba a mis abuelos. / No, (yo) no visitaba a mis abuelos.

19. Were you afraid of monsters?

Yes, I was afraid of monsters. / No, I wasn't afraid of monsters.

Sí, (yo) tenía miedo de los monstruos. / No, (yo) no tenía miedo de los monstruos.

20. Did you want to be an astronaut?

Yes, I wanted to be an astronaut. / No, I didn't want to be an astronaut.

Sí, (yo) quería ser astronauta. / No, (yo) no quería ser astronauta.

Dialogue 18.1

Elisa – Mateo, I want to know what you were like when you were young. Were you as friendly when you were young?

Mateo – Well, I don't know anything about that, but yes, more or less ... I was friendly with everyone. I wasn't shy.

Elisa - You were always cute, right? Because you're very handsome now.

Mateo- Thank you, Elisa. I believe so. I was always cute. That's what my mom says.

Elisa - And what did you like to do? Did you play much with your friends?

Mateo- Well, yes, I always used to play with the same girl. Her name was Susana. She was a very pretty and very nice girl.

Elisa - A girl? Susana?

Mateo - Yes. Susan was a fabulous girl. She was intelligent and always won the games. She used to eat with my family almost every day.

Elisa - A fabulous girl, huh? She always used to go to your house and used to spend time with your family?

Mateo -   Oh, yes. She had long hair and big eyes and...

Elisa -   Well, Mateo. I believe that now I know enough information aboutwhen you were young. It's better to talk about the future. Don't you think?

Chapter 19

Practice 19.1
1. hablé
2. cantó
3. trabajamos
4. bailaron
5. viajaste

Practice 19.2
1. corrí
2. vivió
3. comimos
4. abrieron
5. vendiste

Practice 19.3
1. Who took out the trash?
   I took out the trash.
   (Yo) saqué la basura.
2. What did you play yesterday?
   I played tennis yesterday.
   (Yo) jugué al tenis ayer.
   ¿Qué jugaste ayer? (al tenis)
3. How long did you play the piano?
   I played the piano for three years.
   (Yo) toqué el piano por tres años.
4. How much did you pay for the meal?
   I paid thirty dollars for the meal.
   (Yo) pagué treinta dólares por la comida.
5. Who arrived?
   Miguel and Sara arrived.
   Miguel y Sara llegaron.
6. What did you hand over?
   I handed over my passport.
   (Yo) entregué mi pasaporte.

Practice 19.4
1. Did you play soccer yesterday?
   No, I played baseball yesterday.
   No, (yo) jugué al béisbol ayer.

2. Did you hear the news today?

   Yes, I heard the news today.

   Sí, (yo) oí las noticias de hoy.

3. Who did you hug this morning?

   I hugged my husband/wife this morning.

   (Yo) abracé a mi esposo/a esta mañana.

4. What did you read recently?

   I read an adventure book recently.

   (Yo) leí un libro de aventuras recientemente.

5. Did you enjoy this class?

   Of course I enjoyed this class.

   Claro que sí (yo) gocé esta clase.

6. At what time did this class begin tonight?

   This class began at 7:00 tonight.

   Esta clase comenzó a las siete esta noche.

7. What did you look for in that dictionary?

   I looked for a new word in that dictionary.

   (Yo) busqué una palabra nueva en ese diccionario.

8. Who made a mistake with the information?

   I made a mistake with the information.

   (Yo) me equivoqué con la información.

Practice 19.5

1. What did you brother laugh at?
   My brother laughed at the joke.
   Mi hermano se rió del chiste.
2. Who repeated the new words?
   The students repeated the new words.
   Los estudiantes repitieron las palabras nuevas.
3. How did you feel in class last night?
   I felt very nervious in class last night.
   Me sentí muy nervioso(a) en la clase anoche.
4. How did you all sleep last night?
   We slept very well last night.
   (Nosotros) dormimos muy bien anoche.
5. Who served the meal?
   The waiter served the meal.
   El mesero sirvió la comida.
6. Did you enjoy yourself at the party?
   Yes, I enjoyed myself at the party.
   Sí, (yo) me divertí en la fiesta.
7. What did you all order?
   I ordered a taco; my husband ordered a sandwich.
   (Yo) pedí un taco; mi esposo pidió una torta.

8. Which did you all prefer?

    I preferred the book; my friend preferred the movie.

    (Yo) preferí el libro; mi amigo(a) prefirió la película.

Practice 19.6

1. Did you drive your car to class tonight?

    Yes, I drove my car to class tonight.

    Sí, (yo) conduje mi coche para ir a clase esta noche.

2. Who brought their book to class?

    Everyone brought their books to class.

    Todos trajeron sus libros a clase.

3. Did you have to work today?

    Yes, I had to work today.

    Sí, (yo) tuve que trabajar hoy.

4. What movie did you see last night?

    I saw a romantic movie last night.

    (Yo) vi una película romántica anoche.

5. Where were you all last night?

    We were at home last night.

    (Nosotros) estuvimos en casa anoche.

6. Where did you all go yesterday afternoon?

    Yesterday afternoon we went to the park.

    Ayer por la tarde fuimos al parque.

7. Could you understand the question?

    No I wasn't able to understand the question.

    No, (yo) no pude comprender la pregunta.

8. From whom did you find out the secret?

    I found out the secret from Juana.

    (Yo) supe el secreto de Juana.

9. What did the man say?

    The man said that the store is there.

    El señor dijo que la tienda está allí.

10. Where did you put the documents?

    I put the documents on the table.

    (Yo) puse los documentos en la mesa.

Practice 19.7

The Magic Shell

Every summer my parents, my brother and I used to visit our grandparents that lived in a very small house near the beach. During the days, my brother and I always swam in the ocean while the adults rested in the house playing chess or reading novels. But in the evenings, my grandmother always told us stories of the past. One night, she told us a secret that still fascinates me.

One night during a very long summer, when she was 16 years old, she decided to take a walk along the shore of the ocean. It was 7:00 at night and it was a tranquil night, some minutes after the sunset. While my grandmother was walking along the sand, suddenly she heard a beautiful voice singing slowly a very interesting song. But, my grandmother didn't see anyone on the beach. There was only herself and a shell on the sand. But that shell was very strange, of a very beautiful color ... a light blue with green and red stripes with a yellow circle. My grandmother looked at it more carefully and saw that in that yellow circle, the shell had some very black eyes and a small mouth. At this moment, the shell said to my grandmother, "What thing do you want more than anything in the world? I can give you this thing, but only one... you only have to tell me and I will give it to you right now... here on this beach and in this moment.   You have to decide quickly because I can't stay here for much longer. I am a magic shell and since you found me, you can receive your most important wish in all the world. Tell me, young lady, what do you want? Tell me what is in your heart." Well, my grandmother didn't get scared. She asked the magic shell for a small house near the beach with the man of her dreams inside. And you know what? The shell gave her her wish, and that's how my grandmother met my grandfather, the man of her dreams living in the small house near the beach.

Practice 19.7

1. The grandmother of the narrator lives in the city
   Falso (vive en la playa) = *False (she lives on the beach)*
2. Each evening the grandmother tells stories about the family
   Cierto = *true*
3. The story that the grandmother tells that night is the story of how she met the grandfather.
   Cierto = *true*
4. The grandmother found the shell in a small house near the beach.
   Falso (encontró el caracol en la arena) = *False, (she found the shell on the sand)*
5. The shell could give the grandmother three wishes.
   Falso (pudo darle solo un deseo) = F*alse (he could give her only one wish)*
6. The grandmother was afraid of the shell.
   Falso (no tuvo miedo) = *False (She wasn't afraid)*
7. The grandmother received her wish.
   Cierto = *true*

Practice 19.8

A Visit With A Friend

My name is Carolina. I live in an apartment in Miami and I am a secretary. I work with a very hard working lawyer and I almost never have free time. But, yesterday, finally, I had free time to visit an old friend of mine. She lives in an apartment in the city. I haven't seen her for many years. My friend's name is Teresa and we met ten years ago in the university.

I arrived to her apartment at 10AM. She was as pretty as I remembered. She had long blond hair and big, brown eyes. Her apartment was small but pretty. She likes nature and for that reason there were may plants and flowers in her apartment.

We talked in her apartment for a little while, and afterwards, we decided to go to eat in a restaurant for lunch. We went to a Japanese restaurant because we both like sushi a lot. We sat down at a round table and looked at the menu. It was then when a tall man entered. He was wearing a suit and a dark purple tie. (Dark purple is my friend's favorite color). My friend was looking at him when the man sat down in a chair at the table with us. What a surprise! My friend didn't say anything to me but she began to talk with him. She told him her name and the man told her his. Several minutes passed and I was sitting there in silence watching this very interesting scene.

After a while, the waiter arrived with the drinks. Do you think that their conversation ended that way? I did ... I believed it at that moment. But it wasn't like that! My friend ordered our lunch without consulting me. She didn't talk to me or look at me. The waiter left, and the two continued to talk. It surprised me so much that I didn't say anything. I sat in silence. The two continued to talk with much energy and enthusiasm. The spoke about sports, their travels, their jobs, and meanwhile, I said nothing. We ate together while the two talked more about their interests and their families and their desires for the future. Finally, the waiter brought us the bill. The man thanked her for everything and left. My friend, finally, looked at me and smiled at me.
-"What do you think?," she asked me.
-"What should I think," I asked her, incredulous.
Then she explained everything to me. She had arranged a date with that man over the internet. She was afraid of meeting him in person without another person there to protect her. She decided to have a date with him and a visit with me at the same time.

"What do you think of him?" she asked me.

"I don't know anything about him, " I told her, "But about you, I have a completely different opinion."

I got up from the chair, left money on the table, and I left.

Practice 19.8
1. What is the name of the friend.
    A. Susana
    B. Teresa
    C. Carolina
    D. No menciona el nombre = *(the name isn't mentioned)*
2. Where does the friend live?
    A. en Los Ángeles
    B. en una ciudad en Miami   = *(in a city in Miami)*
    C. en México
    D. en Tejas
3. Where did the two girls go to eat lunch?

    A. en el apartamento de Teresa = *(in Teresa's apartment)*
    B. en un restaurante chino = *(in a Chinese restaurant)*
    C. en la cafetería donde trabaja Carolina = *(in the cafeteria where Carolina works)*
    D. en un restaurante japonés =(in a Japanese restaurant)
4. Who arrived at the restaurant?
    A. Otra amiga de las chicas =(*another friend of the girls'*)
    B. Un hombre bajo = (*a short man*)
    C. Un hombre alto = (*a tall man*)
    D. Una mujer bonita = (*a pretty woman*)

5. Why was the man there and why did he sit down at the same table?
   A. Estuvo allí porque tenía una cita con Teresa = (*He was there because he had a date with Teresa*)
   B. Estuvo allí porque era amigo de Teresa = (*He was there because he was a friend of Teresa's*)
   C. Estuvo allí porque era amigo de Teresa y Carolina de la universidad. =(*He was there because he was a friend of Teresa and Carolina's from the university*).
   D. No menciona por qué estuvo allí. = (*It doesn't mention why he was there*)
6. What did the narrator do at the end of the story?
   A. Hizo una cita con el hombre alto. =(*She made a date with the tall man*)
   B. Recibió un trabajo del hombre y salió con él. = (*She received a job from the man and left with him*)
   C. Continuó su conversación y visita con su amiga. =(*She continued her conversation and visit with her friend*).
   D. Se enojó y salió del restaurante. = (*She got angry and left*)

¡Bien hecho!

Made in the USA
Lexington, KY
02 November 2015